LIVING AMONG THE DEAD

MY GRANDMOTHER'S HOLOCAUST SURVIVAL STORY OF LOVE AND STRENGTH

ADENA BERNSTEIN ASTROWSKY

Living among the Dead. My Grandmother's Holocaust Survival Story of Love and Strength

Featuring the writings of Mania Lichtenstein

Narrative provided by her granddaughter, Adena Bernstein Astrowsky

Copyright © Adena Bernstein Astrowsky, 2020

ISBN 9789493056381 (ebook)

ISBN 9789493056374 (paperback)

ISBN 9789493056596 (hardcover)

ISBN 9789493231450 (audiobook)

Part of the Series Holocaust Survivor True Stories

Publisher: Amsterdam Publishers

info@amsterdampublishers.com

adena.astrowsky@gmail.com

Frontcover: Mania Lichtenstein ('Bubbie') and Adena's mother in Berlin after the Second World War.

All Rights Reserved. No part of this publication may be reproduced or transmitted in any form or by any means, electronic or mechanical, including photocopy, recording or any other information storage and retrieval system, without prior permission in writing from the publisher.

Awards: 2022 IAN Book of the Year Outstanding Non-Fiction Winner; 2020 Readers Favorite Gold Medal Winner in the Non-Fiction Biography genre; First Place medal in the 2020 Royal Dragonfly Book Award Contest in the Biography/Autobiography/Memoir genre.

CONTENTS

Recommendations	ix
Acknowledgments	xv
Introduction	xvii
1. Bubbie	1
2. The World I once knew	13
3. Nechamka	22
4. Family	26
5. Life in Poland	31
6. Russian Control	43
7. Unforgettable Images	46
8. German Occupation	51
9. The Beginning of the End	55
10. Life in the Attic	65
11. A New Ghetto	70
12. One Thousand Remaining	74
13. In the Forest	81
14. Liberation	87
15. My Home	90
16. Looking for a New Home	93
17. Leaving 'Blood-Soaked Europe'	98
18. Moving to a New Country	101
19. My odd Wedding Day	110
20. Righteous Among the Nations	115
21. More of Mania's Writings	120
Postscript	135
Review Request	139
Notes	143
Amsterdam Publishers Holocaust Library	147

"... things that happened years ago keep flashing before my eyes. If they could only be rinsed away with the tears that they cause!"
Mania Lichtenstein

I dedicate this book to my three beautiful children,

Sarah, Zachary, and Gabby.

They are the living reminders that although a total of 11 million people were murdered at the hands of the Nazis, Hitler failed in his quest to completely exterminate Jews from this planet.

May the memories of all those who have perished be for a blessing.

RECOMMENDATIONS

I was honored when asked to read and review Adena Astrowsky's book, *Living among the Dead*. What stood out for me is how different this book is from many of the other Holocaust books. I was most impressed with two things: 1) the amount of important documentary information which is often not known or forgotten, and 2) the details about her grandmother's life in labor camps. I feel it is a very important and well-written book that the world needs to read. As I told Adena, she did a "Mitzvah" (a good deed) for the world by documenting her grandmother's story in such an excellent way.

– **Ben Lesser**, Holocaust Survivor, Author, Speaker, and Founder of Zachor: Holocaust Remembrance Foundation

---

An inspiring story of values and tradition from generation to generation by a granddaughter who has dedicated her life's work to being a prosecutor of victim-crimes. Narrative history of the Holocaust through discussions with her grandmother "Bubbie" who wrote poetry during the Holocaust as well as her thoughts through the years. "Bubbie's" poems, such as *The Nostalgic Past*, could easily be adapted to middle and high school class lesson plans.

—**Jay Levinsohn**, teacher

Even though it is incredibly difficult to read about the soulless cruelty inflicted upon Jews and other groups during World War II, it is imperative that we do so. The idea that the recurrence of the demonization of an entire race could ever happen again should seem not just implausible, but impossible. Tragically, however, we find ourselves in a world reeling from a resurgence of hate and violence. Against this backdrop, Adena Bernstein Astrowsky's *Living among the Dead* can help serve as an important wakeup call.

Kudos to Astrowsky, Mania Lichtenstein's granddaughter, for preserving her grandmother's wartime experiences. "I was in elementary school when I first learned that my grandmother was a Holocaust survivor," says Astrowsky. That early exposure to stories of the unthinkable cruelty inflicted on her grandmother left an indelible mark. Through their eyes, *Living among the Dead* — a collection of Lichtenstein's writings and her granddaughter's observations — becomes a gift of immeasurable importance for us all.

This book should be found in every library from middle school on up. Readers will come away feeling a range of emotions. Mine is of enormous sadness tempered with gratitude and the eternal hope that these lessons are not lost on this and future generations.

— **Linda F. Radke**, President, Story Monsters LLC, formerly Five Star Publications, Inc.

I have twice been gifted the opportunity of helping bring forth the stories of Holocaust survivors — first when I helped write Cantor Leo Fettman's biography (*Shoah: Journey from the Ashes*) and then, more recently, when asked to edit *Living among the Dead*. Understandably, I found both of these experiences to be deeply moving and emotional.

Living among the Dead is Adena Bernstein Astrowsky's loving and careful reflection of passages from her grandmother's private journal that Mania Lichtenstein kept as a way of coping with the memories of what she'd survived in World War II. In addition to these notes written by Mania Lichtenstein, Astrowsky also spent years talking with her grandmother about her experiences, difficult as though many of these conversations were.

So do we need another Holocaust book? The answer becomes obvious when one sees the rise of hate groups. Jews, Christians, Muslims, Hindus, agnostics, and atheists— we are all brothers and sisters. But when hatred and discrimination, born almost entirely from ignorance and fear, enter the mainstream of our lives, we very much need this book.

Living among the Dead is another valuable brick in the "never again" wall that demands constant attention and refortification.

– **Paul M. Howey**, writer and editor

For most Americans alive at the end of WWII, news of the Holocaust came in the form of photographs in USA's most popular magazine - LIFE – heaps of skeletal remains and barely human faces staring into cameras General Eisenhower ordered to document Nazi horrors in "concentration camps." A few years later, the "best-seller" was by the brilliant teenage daughter of a German-Jewish family hiding in Holland. Still read in many American schools, *The Diary of Anne Frank* ends without revealing the terrible fate we now know all but Anne's father shared with "the six million." After half a century, we have come to know the limits of these best-known sources. Most Jews killed were not from Germany, but Eastern Europe. And most did not die in "camps", but in their lifelong communities, slaughtered by *Einsatzgruppen*, then buried in pits, up to tens of thousands a day.

The genius of *Living Among the Dead* is not just that it is one of only a few memoirs to describe this form of death – 20,000 Jews slaughtered in Polish city of Wlodzimierz alone – but also conveys how Jews lived in Eastern Europe, which large numbers of today's Jews identify as their place of origin.

Ostensibly co-written by two generations of authors – grandmother and grand-daughter, both self-designated "Memorial Candles" – there are actually three narrators: (1) the 17-year-old girl who cheats death by what she calls "fate" and we can see as an uncanny ability to always align herself with good people who can help her; (2) the mature woman she became, with the wisdom to flee "blood-soaked" Europe for Canada, then immigrate to America, working as a bookkeeper, becoming an avid reader of literary classics in multiple languages, persisting in writing her memoirs past loss of eyesight; and (3) her lawyer grand-daughter who persisted through years of sometimes difficult interviews, then skilfully constructed a narrative, beginning with the B'nai Mitzvot of her twins, days after death of their beloved B-Bubbie – the quintessential "survivor" who (as the author wrote) "wanted to be sure the rest of the world did not forget the beauty of the culture her family enjoyed before it was so despicably destroyed." Wonderful book - a treasure of individual strength, family love, community solidarity and Jewish History.

– **Marcia Ruth**, retired writer and editor

Using both her own words and her grandmother's, Astrowksy weaves the story of survival against all odds during the Holocaust. Before I had even finished the book, I felt I knew "Bubby" and could hear her unwavering voice through her poetry and her amazing story of war and strife in Eastern Europe.

– **Kimberly Klett,** Museum Teacher 2003-04, United States Holocaust Memorial Museum and Executive Deputy Director, Educators' Institute for Human Rights

Living among the Dead is a riveting, heart-felt glimpse into one young girl's path into and out of the Holocaust. A childhood once filled with joy and innocence was replaced with utter despair as she lost her entire family and had to learn to survive on her own. While her survival was nothing short of a miracle, the true significance of this story is the ultimate triumph of good over evil through a life well lived, and a legacy secured.

Living among the Dead transforms the study of the Holocaust from a distant event to a personal journey. As a teacher, I believe reading this book will help my students develop a richer, more intimate understanding of this period in history, and better equip them to do the important work of sharing the lessons of the Holocaust with future generations.

– **Sarah Armistead**, M.P.A., 8th Grade History Teacher

Living among the Dead by Adena Bernstein Astrowsky is a memoir that features the writings of her grandmother Mania Lichtenstein who survived the atrocities of the Holocaust. Astrowsky skilfully weaves her grandmother's poetry and personal reflections into a narrative providing context and connection with the audience. From sharing her grandmother's story, we learn through a first-hand account the horrific experiences she endured to survive, and through her survival we learn lessons of courage, resiliency, and the value of life.

The experiences that Astrowsky provides are more than a family history. It is a story of culture and meaning showing the importance of relationships and family during challenging and rewarding times. Many of the personal memories focused on the people that were involved; those who were lost, those who survived, and the family that surrounded her. It is easy to fathom how one would fall into despair as a result of these experiences; however, when we learn of how Lichtenstein chose to live her life, we understand why it was important for her to have hope and persevere.

World War II was more than seven decades ago and many who lived during that time have passed away. In order to understand history's impact is to have first hand accounts of those who lived it; it is also important to never forget the events of the holocaust so that history does not repeat itself. *Living among the Dead* is an excellent book that does both. Not only does Astrowsky share these important perspectives, she provides a wonderful tribute to her grandmother who loved her family.

– **Paul Becker**, Secondary Language Arts Coach, Scottsdale Unified School district

ACKNOWLEDGMENTS

I would like to express my heartfelt gratitude to the many people that helped to memorialize my grandmother's story of survival. Creating a book such as this requires a lot of time outside of my full-time job and away from my family. I would like to begin by thanking my husband, Brad, and my children, Sarah, Zachary, and Gabby, for their patience and love while I spent many evenings and weekends working on this project. I missed quite a few activities and social gatherings to sit at my laptop to research and write. It is with them in mind, however, that I decided to take on this project.

I would also like to thank my mother, Jeanie Bernstein, for spending so much time with me as I went through the entire story of her mother's survival. She was very helpful in filling in many of the post-war gaps. Also, questions developed along the way that required additional knowledge of specific details that my father (Allan Bernstein), sisters (Joanna and Corinne), and their families were able to provide. I thank them as well.

Several people helped translate letters my grandmother wrote in Polish and Yiddish. I would like to thank my friend, Joanna Jablonski and her mother, Eva Morris, for their assistance in translating the letter and card in Polish. For the two letters in Yiddish, I thank Levi Levertov, Jeff Miller, and Etty Sims for all their help.

A profound thank you to the staff at Yad Vashem and the U.S. Holocaust Memorial Museum. Both museums provided many resources and assistance throughout the writing of this book. I would like to specifically thank Maria Sehen, with Yad Vashem, for her assistance in processing Janina's nomination for consideration to be included in the "Righteous People Among the Nations" list and for her additional help with locating information about my grandmother's hometown. Maria also put me in touch with a childhood friend of my grandmother's, Genia Seifert, who provided additional details which helped me understand my grandmother's childhood. I am so grateful to my college friend, Shira Gafni, who met with Genia in Israel and spent time at her home asking her many questions on my behalf.

I am forever grateful to Marcia Ruth, for her extraordinary insight and who was able to contribute so many historical facts to this book. Also, I would like to thank Paul Howey who helped edit the original manuscript before it was submitted to Amsterdam Publishers for consideration. Many people volunteered to read an advanced copy of this book and provide an honest review. I am thankful to all of you for your time, support, and words.

Finally, I am eternally grateful to Liesbeth Heenk at Amsterdam Publishers for agreeing to publish this book. From the moment we had our first Skype conversation, I knew this book was in good hands and we would develop a wonderful relationship. With the publication of this book we hope to remind each new generation to Never Forget.

INTRODUCTION

Adena and her grandmother on the beach (1974).

My name is Adena Bernstein Astrowsky, oldest granddaughter of Mania Lichtenstein. My Jewish name is Rivka Nechama. I was named after my grandmother's two sisters, Rivka and Nechamka, both of whom perished in the Holocaust. I have always felt a strong connection to both women, not only because of our shared name but also because of the stories my grandmother told me. Writing this book allowed me to learn the details of her survival (she was known to her family as Bubbie), to think deeply about the odds she had to overcome, and to truly see her in the way she had come to see her mother — as a hero.

I was in elementary school when I first learned that my grandmother was a Holocaust survivor. Even as young as I was then, I knew the Holocaust was a horrendous and unthinkable time in the world's history, and that she was very fortunate to have survived it. But, I must admit, I really didn't think much more about it until I was in middle school when I began asking her questions about her experiences. None of my questions, however, were answered easily. In fact, learning the details of my grandmother's survival was never easy.

I remember studying world history in high school and preparing a list of questions for her. Of course, I was a typically impatient teenager who didn't have endless hours to sit and listen to the whole story.

I wanted my grandmother to answer my specific questions as quickly and succinctly as possible. But she always found it hard to give me simple answers.

Admittedly, my questions probably weren't worded well, but it seemed that a question about one topic would lead her to talk about several other topics. I guess she didn't want me to leave thinking that a single piece of information could represent the whole story. Or it could be the details and events were so intertwined that it was hard for her to separate out the facts I was searching for.

Looking back on my adolescent expectations, I came to understand why this was an impossible task for my grandmother. Each story involved multiple details that needed to be shared in order to answer what I presumed to be a 'simple' question.

What thwarted my efforts the most were the nightmares I came to learn she would endure, sometimes for weeks, after having shared with me her experiences. It's a side effect common to many victims of trauma: recounting the awful event often forces them to suffer all over again. This was not something I wanted for her. Yet, she was not to be dissuaded.

Bubbie held steadfast to the strong desire that her family know its roots. She emphasized this time and again as her children had children, and those children had children, with the Holocaust becoming ever further removed from the consciousness of each generation. As she watched this happen, it became even more imperative for her that we know our shared history.

My grandmother's purpose in this was not for us to dwell on the horrific details. Rather, she wanted to enrich our lives through knowledge of the past. In other words, she did not believe we were aware of what we were missing by not knowing the story of her survival, and of those who did not survive the Holocaust. It is my hope — with the writing of this book — that her descendants and others will know not just the horrors wrought by the Nazis, but also the beauty of the lives created by the Jews.

And so, over the years, my grandmother chose the medium of writing to cope with and express her feelings and emotions. Often at night, when she couldn't sleep, she would sit at a desk alone in her bedroom and write. Even in the later years, when her vision became diminished, she continued writing with the aid of an Elmo magnifying machine. Writing was her therapy. For me, too, the benefits were enormous, as I was better able to understand what she was trying to tell me.

Through her writing, I was able to piece together the story of her survival. Bubbie wanted to be sure the rest of the world did not forget the beauty of the culture she and her family enjoyed before it was so despicably destroyed. She wrote:

> *So much idle time, only my mind keeps working...*

> *So many memories of years gone by,*
> *crowding my mind.*
>
> *I must talk,*
> *but who is there to listen?*
> *Those who would relate and understand*
> *are either gone or far away.*
> *So I 'talk' by writing,*
> *though I am the only one that listens.*
> *It is the second best thing for me to ease my mind.*

I can only guess why she considered it the second best thing. Perhaps because she had no one to talk with about it, which she would probably have preferred.

I was in law school when I learned of the Shoah Foundation, an organization founded by Steven Spielberg to help present and future generations learn about the Holocaust. It does this in part by collecting and preserving the personal stories of survivors and other witnesses of the Holocaust.

I arranged for someone from the Foundation to interview my grandmother and video record her testimony. I watched all four hours of her testimony several times. Doing so greatly enhanced my appreciation of what she'd endured — and, in truth, continued to endure. That experience further confirmed my decision to write her story.

When I began writing, she was still alive and living near me. I was able to interview her often about specific topics I felt were either confusing or needed more clarification and details.

Again, asking her questions wasn't always easy, nor could I expect a simple, straightforward answer; but when I brought my young children — Sarah, Zachary, and Gabby — with me, it seemed to help her stay focused.

She answered my questions carefully because she could see that they, too, were trying to understand her story as fourth-generation survivors.

Zachary, Gabby, Bubbie, and Sarah.

Zachary, Gabby, Bubbie, and Sarah.

Two months after an earlier version of this book was published, my beloved grandmother passed away. May her memory be a blessing.

I have thought a lot about why this project is important to me. At first, my answer was simple: to memorialize the details of my grandmother's survival for our children and all future generations to read and understand.

We've all heard the saying: *We must never forget so that it never happens again.* I believe that my generation holds the power of

'Never Again' by making sure the next generation will indeed 'Never Forget.'

I continue to believe and hope that whatever we learn from one genocide can help us, G-d willing, prevent the next one.

I have long felt what psychologist Dina Wardi describes in her book, *Memorial Candles: Children of the Holocaust*, when she discusses what it's like to be a family member self-selected to be the one to carry the memory and the legacy of those who did or did not survive.

I know that — as I've grown in my knowledge of the Holocaust and lived more years as a mother to three now teenage children — I have also become more aware of the anti-Semitism that still festers in countries throughout the world. I also know that genocide continues for other groups who, like the Jews about 80 years ago, are being murdered simply for their ethnicity.

Today, according to the United States Holocaust Memorial Museum, "The world is experiencing the largest humanitarian crisis since the end of World War II and the Holocaust. Syria, Afghanistan, and South Sudan account for more than half the 25 million refugees around the world today." Many of these refugees are fleeing situations not unlike those faced by Jews throughout Europe prior to the war.

Thus, it was especially poignant in April 2019 when Temple Solel (my place of worship in Paradise Valley, Arizona) brought in a refugee family that had fled war-torn Syria through the Syrian Refugee Program. They were a family of four — mom and dad, son and daughter. They moved to the United States because their government was turning on its own people. The Syrian police shot at the father. They did not feel that they would survive staying in Syria. The Syrian Refugee office in Jordan that helped them emigrate chose the United States as their destination of safety. This family knew very little of Western culture, and even though they had been living in the United States for two years at the time they spoke at my temple, only the children could speak English.

The dilemma they were in — and the opportunity they were offered here in the United States — reminded me of my grandmother and the basic skills required just to survive, such as speaking the local language.

In addition to learning Polish in school and Yiddish at home, my grandmother would go on to learn Russian, German, French, and English out of a need to survive and provide for her family.

Similar to the refugee family that moved to America and had to learn English, my grandmother, too, was forced to learn new languages in order to assimilate, raise her children, maintain a job, converse with neighbors, and so on.

My hope in writing this book is to draw attention to people being persecuted for who they are. My goal is to foster understanding and empathy, especially when relating to a generation nearly gone, by telling my grandmother's story of hope and survival when all else was lost.

My grandmother had one word to describe how she survived the Holocaust, the genocide that murdered her entire family:

As a survivor of the Holocaust, I am very often asked this question: "How did you survive?" Indeed, how? I, the youngest of the family, shy and insecure, far from being brave. I could answer it with one word: Fate. I was meant to survive three pogroms, which eliminated the town's about 26,000 Jews. - Mania Lichtenstein, 1995

And she asked the same question that has been asked by so many for the past eight decades: Why did the Nazis murder millions of Jewish men, women, and children, Gypsies, Jehovah's Witnesses, Seventh-day Adventists, homosexuals, political resisters and dissidents, and others?

Why

I wake up and cry,
My aching heart is uttering—why?
Why did they do this to us?
I cannot stop the tears;
That keep running down my face,
For the pain in my heart remains.

Mania Lichtenstein, 1980

What follows is the story of my grandmother.

1

BUBBIE

Bubbie was a daughter, sister, wife, mother of two, grandmother of five, great-grandmother of ten. And she was a Holocaust Survivor. This is about her life — or at least the bits and pieces of that life that she shared with me in conversations and in her writings. She spoke of her earliest childhood memories and of living through the Holocaust.

Her story is now history. But, because she somehow miraculously survived horrific events and unimaginable degradation, her family, her faith, and her hope — they survive, too.

Like most members of my generation, born three decades after the end of World War II, I came to this story with almost no *real* understanding of the plight of Jews in the Holocaust, much less that of my own grandmother.

Adena held by her grandmother, right after she was born, April 1971

I grew up in a lovely home surrounded by family and friends. I was involved in many activities at school and by all measures was a normal, happy kid. But growing up I couldn't help but notice what is often called "presence of absence" on my mother's side of the family.

When we got together with family on my father's side, there were so many aunts and uncles and first cousins.

One of my cousins nicknamed me '#9' and I refer to him to this day as '#5', signifying the birth order of first cousins on my father's side. But on my mother's side, I grew up with only one aunt, who got married in my early teens.

While I was in high school, she and my uncle had two daughters. And, of course, there was my grandmother, my Bubbie. So, compared to my father's side, my mother's side of the family was very small. Sometime during my high school years, I began to grow curious about the significance of this difference.

As my grandmother's first-born grandchild, I was very fortunate to have spent a lot of time with her throughout my life.

Shortly after I was born in Maryland, my family moved back to Canada (my parents had lived in Montreal prior to my birth) and moved into the same apartment building as my grandmother in Cote St. Luc, Montreal.

Each day my mom and I sat in my bedroom and looked out the window waiting for my grandmother to return from her job as a bookkeeper. When she got home, she would often take me from our ground level apartment to hers on an upper floor where we would spend time together playing and talking.

This allowed my parents to spend some time alone together when my father returned from work. Now, as a parent of three, I can appreciate how important those moments can be without a toddler running around! (On a side note, if you look at photos taken of me during these early years, you can see a noticeable weight gain because my grandmother took this time to feed me cookies that I enjoyed so very much!)

My sisters were born within the next few years and we soon moved to a home in Dollard des Ormeaux, a suburb of Montreal.

I have warm and wonderful memories of these times I spent with my grandmother. I remember playing a game in which she'd spin me around in her green laundry basket. She would also make dolls out of towels for my sisters and me, something she continued to do for my children when they were toddlers. She also drew pictures of pussycats, something she later taught my children how to do.

My favorite memory? That would have to be the sugar cookies she'd make from a recipe she remembered from when she lived in Germany. I can close my eyes and still see her using the same cookie cutters over and over to make these delicious treats.

In 1976, the election in Quebec involved three political parties. The victorious party ('Partie Quebecquoise' led by Premier Rene Leveque) won with 40 percent of the vote. They were a separatist party whose goal was for Quebec to secede from Canada and operate as an independent country. They installed a plethora of new rules, many of them about language making it harder for businesses to operate. To send a child to an English-speaking school, for example, at least one parent had to have attended one of these schools.

For many reasons, including political ones, my parents moved to the United States in 1978. They had to file application papers, and my aunt on my father's side who lived in New York had to vouch for us, in order for us to be allowed to enter the United States. Therefore, because of the political and economic issues in Montreal, my family ended up moving to Arizona.

After living in Arizona for five years, my mother became a citizen and then filed the government papers necessary for her to move my grandmother to Arizona, which she eventually did in 1985. My father owned his own dental business and my grandmother went to work there as the firm's bookkeeper. My grandmother always lived close to us, and so was able to be with us for all religious holidays, some of our vacations, and other important family occasions.

Growing up so close to her was indeed a blessing as it allowed me to spend a lot of valuable time with her, getting to know her, and creating some fabulous memories that continue to nourish me to this day.

My grandmother was an avid reader. She loved reading books, especially those by James Michener, Leon Uris, Fyodor Dostojevsky. After finishing *War and Peace* by Leo Tolstoy, my grandmother joked with my mother about how difficult it was to pronounce the long names used in the book as they went "on and on."

Bubbie also loved music, especially if composed by Johann Strauss II and Frédéric Chopin. She also enjoyed operas such as *The Merry Widow*, *Rigoletto*, and *La Bohème*. My mother told me she recalled being a teenager in the 1950s when my grandmother would ask her to teach her the "cha-cha" and jitterbug. She just loved to dance!

With the birth of my children, my grandmother said it really brought home to her how — despite the unimaginable magnitude of his hatred and violence — Hitler had failed to wipe all Jews off the planet.

The lone survivor in her family, she had given birth to two daughters, who in turn birthed her five grandchildren. And then those grandchildren grew up and had babies of their own. She was a great-grandmother to even more little human beings. When she thought about that, she was visibly moved.

Not only I, but my three children, too, were fortunate to spend a lot of their childhood with her. They experienced the same doll-making activities, the drawing of pussycats on paper, and eating sugar cookies shaped by the same cookie cutters she'd used when I was a child.

Each December we would go visit her on her birthday with a bouquet of sunflowers — a flower that always reminded her of her childhood home and garden. Running down the hallway, we would see her standing outside her apartment door waiting for us. My children would often yell out, "Happy Birthday, B-Bubbie," to which she would vehemently shush them because although her true birthday was in December, she still used the fake (or inherited) birthday of March on all her paperwork. And although WWII was long over, she was still nervous someone would find out or a Nazi was lurking nearby.

It even humored us to see the birthday fliers posted in the elevators and on the walls of the assisted living facility she spent her last few years at, listing her name under the "March Birthdays" for residents that month.

Occasionally though, I did experience impatience when my children would complain of being 'starving.' Invariably, these incidents evoked in me memories of my grandmother's description of how, during the war, she would be forced to go days, even weeks, with little to no food and scarcely any water.

I would feel myself tensing up as I reminded them that they certainly were *not* "starving." And I would tell them how their great-grandmother once spent fifteen days hiding in an attic with hardly a bite of anything and only a sip of stale water to drink. Of course, they grew tired of this response and I tried to remind them of their great-grandmother's survival story each and every time they complained of starvation.

A few years before my grandmother passed away, I began thinking about the need to collect all the poetry and prose she had written. I wanted to make sure everything was kept safely for my children and their children and their children's children.

As I read through her writings, I realized there were many details of her survival that she had not captured on paper. With that in mind, I watched her taped interview with Steven Spielberg's Shoah Foundation, and began connecting this verbal storyline to her own writings.

Understandably, most survivors have a difficult time talking about what they witnessed and experienced. This was certainly the case with my grandmother. As I mentioned earlier, she never offered a simple answer to any of my questions. So, I started spending more time with her every chance I had, with my laptop in tow, asking her questions and documenting her answers, trying to fill in the blanks.

On one such occasion, my son Zachary and I joined her for dinner in the little restaurant at her assisted-living facility to get more details on a particular topic. I don't remember now what that topic was, but I do recall that instead of discussing it, she decided to tell Zachary and me all about the sunflowers that grew wildly in her family's garden when she was a child and how, even to this day, sunflowers reminded her of her childhood home. To her, they were a beloved symbol of all that was good before the war. It was a beautiful, and meaningful, digression in our conversation.

Once the draft version was complete, my kids and I brought a copy to her. I remember how emotional she got and how thankful she was because *her* story, *her* history was now documented and preserved for all the generations that come after her.

There is something simultaneously poignant and incredibly important about not forgetting these stories. Second and third generation survivors need to assume the responsibility for keeping these stories alive.

Gabby, Bubbie, Adena, Sarah, and Zachary.

That realization was the spark that led me to author the first version of this book. My grandmother passed away two months after she received her copy.

Some family members speculated that she continued living until the publication of the book because "knowing your roots" was so important to her.

The last night she was in the hospital before moving to hospice care, my twins, Sarah and Zachary, visited her. Their B'nai Mitzvah was approximately one week away.

Although my grandmother was not a particularly religious person, she asked them to recite for her their Torah portions or at least as much as they could recall from memory. I was enormously proud that they'd both learned their sections so well. While they chanted it in Hebrew, she closed her eyes and listened to them sing.

I don't know what she was thinking, but there was no mistaking the serenity in her expression. She seemed at peace. Perhaps she felt blessed being able to hear their portions, knowing it was most unlikely that she would be able to attend their B'nai Mitzvah in person.

Perhaps, hearing the chanting of the Hebrew reminded her of a time long ago. Or perhaps she knew she was dying and there was something comforting about hearing her great-grandchildren chanting as they prepared to become a Bar and Bat Mitzvah, thus keeping alive a religious tradition and culture of our family and ancestors. I do not know the answer, of course; but as I watched her close her eyes, and listen to my children and to me, she seemed at peace.

Three days before Sarah's and Zachary's B'nai Mitzvah, she died. The Friday after she passed, we attended her funeral in the morning where each of my children gave a eulogy.

"Hello, I am Sarah Astrowsky," my daughter began, "Mania's great-granddaughter. My great-grandmother is very special to me. She is my hero. I look up to her so much. What I learned from her is to never give up and keep trying. Just because something happened doesn't make you quit. It makes you grow as a person, which she showed us based on what she went through. It was truly heartbreaking when I learned of her death. She is in a better place now and she gets to see her parents, husband, and sisters that she misses a lot. She is looking down on us and is very proud of us all. This gives me a special feeling that I know she will be right beside me — even during difficult times. I love you so much B-Bubbie and I am so lucky I had the privilege to meet you because you are truly my hero!"

My other daughter then said, "I'm Gabby, B-Bubbie's great-granddaughter. When I think of the word 'B-Bubbie,' the first things that come to my mind are strength, hope, love, and beauty. Strength for all the hard times that she had to go through. Hope for believing in goodness and good to come. Love for her helpers. And beauty is not just outside; it is inside as well, and the beauty inside her shined all the time. I miss her a lot. I miss her dearly. But now she is up in heaven with the rest of her family. With G-d at her side. May her memory be a blessing. I will always remember all the songs and teachings I learned from her. I love you, B-Bubbie."

My son Zachary's eulogy could not be found, but he wrote this beautiful dedication: "My great-grandma, better known as B-Bubbie, always spread love regardless of losing her sight or living through the worst times imaginable. Quite literally, my great-grandma has been through hell. What amazes me to this day is what would have happened if she never survived the Holocaust? I wouldn't be alive, and this book would never have been written. However, the most important fact is that so many other lives would not have been impacted by her sense of love.

My great-grandma touched so many people in times of fear and happiness. Every time I visited, her face would light up even though, as she got older, she had no idea what I looked like.

Putting myself in her shoes, I could never imagine what life would be like when all I see is darkness, but that's what makes my great-grandma so special. She would patiently wait for my visits and took such pleasure in talking to me and making me smile.

My B-Bubbie gave my family and me the chance to impact others which is why I will never stop loving her. Even though she is gone, her stories and life live on through her family and descendants. I breathe and walk among others because of her.

It tears me apart knowing that I can't tell her how grateful I am, but I believe she has always known that I loved her overwhelmingly. Although I've known her as the great-grandma who pinches my cheeks and sang me lullabies, even when I was in middle school, I did not know how strong a woman she was.

My great-grandma made me realize to always love because we weren't born to hate, and for this, I will try my hardest to spread joy. I hope she knew that her life has brought more meaning to my world and everyone else's."

I spoke, too, ending my eulogy: "It is heartbreaking and devastating to know she is no longer with us. But then I remember that she hasn't seen her parents and sisters in 27, 225 days, and I am comforted in knowing that she is resting peacefully with them. May her memory be a blessing."

This photo is of the stones my children left at her gravesite following the funeral. Gabby drew a picture of a pussycat that my grandmother taught her how to draw. Sarah quoted the Phil Collins song, 'You'll Be in My Heart,' that he wrote for the movie *Tarzan*. She drew some hearts and wrote, "I love you" on the backside of the rock. Zachary decided to leave his rock unmarked because, in his view, rocks symbolize peace and adventure since they move on from place to place—and he didn't want to deface the beautiful rock he picked out.

That night, we lit the Shabbat candles at temple in celebration of the twins' B'nai Mitzvah. Rabbi Linder talked about how, in Judaism, the need to celebrate life through an event such as a Bar or Bat Mitzvah takes priority over mourning the dead. Quite frankly, it was one of the most emotionally difficult times of my life.

Following those Friday night Shabbat services, we hosted a dinner for our out-of-town friends and family where Sarah and Zachary opened a time capsule box that I'd created at my baby shower when I was pregnant with them.

The very last item they took out of the time capsule was a letter from my grandmother in which she'd written:

> *Adena, Brad, and the new additions,*
> *2003 seems like a very long time ago,*
> *There were wishes, hopes, and prayers,*
> *and knocking on my table of wood.*
> *A year of great expectations,*
> *pink and blue decorations.*
> *Be healthy, happy, and good,*
> *True to our expectations!*
>
> Love, Great Grand Bubbie.

It was so surreal that this, her last communication with us, was just two days after she had passed. While her original intention was for her great-grandchildren to call her 'G-Bubbie' for Grand Bubbie, when the kids were old enough to talk, they came up with the name 'B-Bubbie', and that nickname stuck.

As I write this many years later, it's still so hard for me to believe that she's no longer with us. My grandmother's need for us to know our roots, however, still rings loud and true for me today, as people are still being discriminated against and persecuted simply for who they are.

By knowing your roots and remembering your history, it is my hope that we will all do our part to help achieve peace and to prevent future genocides.

Adena and her grandmother. The photo was taken February 4, 2017, approximately one month before she passed away.

2
THE WORLD I ONCE KNEW

The World I Once Knew

I think of the world that once existed,
And almost in an instant vanished.
We were kids in loving homes, well cared for,
And were happy as kids could be.
We played mostly outdoors, summer or winter,
Invented our own simple games,
We had no modern games known today,
And were much more content than kids of today.
Until... a phantom, a nightmare most evil,
Had befallen our own little world,
Destroyed, tore to pieces, pulled all roots out,
And in two mass graves had it buried.
I sadly remember and long for it.

Mania Lichtenstein, October 26, 2006

My grandmother adored her sisters and tried to emulate them whenever she could. If one of them read a book, she had to read the same book. She said she found that books (and movies) "opened a door for me to an enchanted world." She added that many of her friends could not afford such a luxury as seeing a movie.

And so, when she saw one, which was not often, the whole class would surround her the next day and ask her questions about it. She wrote, "Embellishing and improvising, I told them its story."

Genia Seifert, one of my grandmother's childhood friends described her to me as a 'sweetheart' and a 'good person.'

My grandmother believed that one of the things that contributed to her shyness was her mother's brother who would bombard her with questions and testing her intellect. And while she may have known the answers, she felt worthless and was often too paralyzed to answer him.

"He made a bad impact on my life — may he rest in peace," she wrote years later. "He wanted me to fail."

Her uncle's cruel behavior unfortunately had a negative effect on my grandmother that would last a long time. Eventually, thank goodness, she outgrew it and came to realize that she was smarter than he wanted her to believe.

Mania's father was Gershon Tisch, but his children knew him simply as 'Papa.' Like other men in those days, he was not given to displaying his emotions nor sharing his thoughts, but his deeds spoke louder than his words to my grandmother. She felt his love through his smile when she did something funny or silly.

Gershon and Katya

Gershon owned a drugstore and Bubbie thought of him as a typical father. Each day he rode his bicycle to and from work — nobody owned a car during those times — and Bubbie remembered fondly meeting Papa regularly on the street corner near a Gothic church on his way home from work. From there they would go to the candy shop on the corner where he would treat her to a candy or chocolate. She was the youngest of her siblings, a 'brat' she would say, and yet she always felt special to her parents.

Bubbie described her father as a clean-shaven, slender man who smoked cigarettes and was not very tall. Compared to the Hasidic Jews who wore black hats, black coats, and *tzitzit* (knotted ritual fringes or tassels, worn as an undergarment by Orthodox Jews), Bubbie remembered him as being rather modern.

In fact, her Papa was very modern for his time, wearing a derby hat and a suit to work and in winter, a handsome coat. At home, he spoke either Yiddish or Polish, and while he was not overly affectionate with his children, his smile and attention to Bubbie's antics spoke volumes to her of his love.

In conducting research for this book, a woman at Yad Vashem, Israel's memorial to those affected by the Holocaust, put me in contact with Genia Seifert. Through Shira Gafni, one of my college friends, I was able to communicate with Genia, and learn that she and Bubbie were friends from school.

Additionally, Genia's father Yosef was a good friend of Gershon, who was regarded as knowing a lot about medicine. Once, Genia got bitten by a dog, and instead of taking Genia to see Gershon, he came to her to treat her.

The name of Mania's mother was Gitel (Yiddish) or Gitla (Polish), but she preferred to be called by her Russian name, Katya. Her children called her *Mamuniu*, which is Yiddish for 'mom.'

She described herself as a typical Jewish mother full of heart and soul. Bubbie told me her mother stayed at home to raise her children. She was very caring and proud of her children who always came first in her world. However, Bubbie admitted that, as a child, she did not fully appreciate her mother's good intentions or her caring nature. It wasn't until much later that she began to regard her Mamuniu as a true hero.

Bubbie teared up as she and I discussed her mother. She asked daily for her mother's forgiveness for not acknowledging her true goodness. Then, as our conversation continued, Bubbie's mood would lighten as she recounted a story from her childhood about the weekly Thursday night baking to prepare for the Sabbath.

Bubbie had to go to bed early on school nights, and Thursdays were no exception. But she had a sweet tooth and would always ask to stay up for the cookies and cakes that would soon be coming out of the oven. Of course, they wouldn't be done baking until well after bedtime, so her mother would tell Bubbie to go to bed, promising that she would wake her as soon as the sweets were done. But it never happened.

Every Friday morning, Bubbie would get out of bed and scream at her mother, demanding to know why she did not wake her up. And every Friday morning, her mother would have a new excuse.

Bubbie, by the way, was adept at transitioning between personal memories and facts that helped to give the memories context as we talked. So, on this occasion, without skipping a beat, she began telling me how families baked everything except for bread. For that, she said, there was a local baker who made bread the old-fashioned way, and people preferred to buy his delicious rye bread.

On Thursdays, her mother always went to the local store to buy luxury items, such as cheese. Many families kept kosher in their homes, meaning they would not eat dairy and meat together — some families even used a different set of dishes for dairy than the set of dishes for meals including meat.

According to Jewish law, there are three basic elements of keeping kosher: (1) avoiding any non-kosher animals (fish that don't have fins and scales, land animals that do not both chew their cud and have cleft hooves, and most birds), (2) avoiding eating meat and dairy together, and (3) only eating meat that was slaughtered in a certain way, and drained of blood.

For my grandmother, every meal during the week included meat, except Thursdays when they ate dairy instead. For the dairy meal, they had pierogies filled with blueberries and sour cream, dairy-based soup, and pudding, which was a new food at the time.

Then Bubbie shifted the conversation again, and began describing her mother as a modern, stylish and elegant woman who cared about her looks. And while she was typical in comparison to other mothers at the time, Katya was different in many ways. She owned many hats and high-heeled shoes that my grandmother would try on and model when left alone in the house. Bubbie wrote, "My reflection in the mirror pleased me greatly."

Bubbie's mother cared about the family's home, insisting that their hand-me-down furniture be reupholstered, so it would at least appear to be modern and new. And she also loved to dance, teaching Bubbie different steps in the kitchen.

Delightfully as we spoke, Bubbie remembered all the dance steps and all the melodies of the songs her mother loved. Bubbie also spoke of the pride she felt for her mother, the sort of pride one gains from seeing a parent from a distance, as a person rather than a parent.

Women of her mother's generation did not typically hold jobs outside the home, but Katya was an exception and worked in a pharmacy before getting married, and Katya enjoyed the prestige that came with working in the pharmacy, where she learned to read and interpret the doctors' handwriting on prescriptions.

Many of the Christian adults at that time were illiterate. Jewish males, however, had to become literate by the age of thirteen so they could perform their Bar Mitzvah. During this time increasing numbers of Jewish women were also becoming literate, like Katya, who was one of the leaders in this movement for more education. She helped explain to the patients who could not read what their doctors had ordered on their prescriptions.

Gershon and Gitel 'Katya' Tisch

Bubbie had two older sisters. "Having sisters makes you important and makes you belong somewhere," she told me.

Rivka was the oldest and Mania's elder by more than eight years. She was Bubbie's idol, her 'shining star,' and she sought to emulate her whenever she could. Bubbie remembered Rivka as being a member of the town's elite. She completed the equivalent of high school known as a *gymnasium* in Poland, where she took language classes in Latin, English, French, Ukrainian, and Polish, as well as Ancient History. Instead of waiting for Prince Charming after finishing school, as most girls did at the time, Rivka left for nearby Lvóv to find work as a teacher. And when told that there were no opportunities available in Lvóv, she attended a business college there and studied to become a bookkeeper.

Rivka came home after graduating. A point of pride for Bubbie's mother was that Rivka, while studying out on her own, had also learned household chores and could now make pancakes.

Surprisingly, because girls were not given priority over boys for employment, Rivka landed a job in a Polish company that was related to the pharmacy business. The owner frequently praised Rivka and told her what a good job she was doing.

My dearest sister Rivka

I idolized her beyond words. At the age of 27, in one instant, she, together with the rest of the family, have gone from my life. For many years, I tried not to think of the gone by. It was easier not to.

So many times when she came to my mind, I conscientiously brushed the thought aside. Thinking of her was painful, so I gave myself a temporary reprieve.

Today is Shabbat Hagadol, the Sabbath before Passover, the day she was born. Her birthday was celebrated on April 14.

In those days it was not customary to have a birthday celebration; it was only acknowledged among the family. It was different though in Rivka's case. In retrospect, I seem to understand why.

Like a debutante, being the oldest daughter, she was to be presented. It became an annual affair. It was very exciting to see her friends arrive. They were the finest educated youths, the elite of our town's young. My mother was gloating, as each young man greeted her 'Madame Tysz,' bowed, and kissed her hand, which was the custom then. My mother loved romp.

Rivka was my mentor, my idol, and I so much wanted to be like her. I clearly felt her love for me as well. We once had to write an essay in school and I chose to write about her and what she meant to me. I titled it 'Gwiazda Przewodnia' or 'my guiding star.' It was recognized as the best essay in class, for I wrote it from my heart.

From 1939-1941, the Russians occupied our part of Poland. During that period, she got married to Munia Szafir. Her happiness did not last long. Hitler was threatening Europe's peace and the Russians proceeded to mobilize.

Seven months after their wedding, he was enlisted. She was so crushed. It was chaotic in the early stages of the war. Some managed to desert and return home.

For days I stood with her on the street corner, staring into the horizon, lest he too might appear. It did not happen. In 1941 Hitler invaded again and absolved us from all life's worries.

My dear sister, I will always love you and you will always remain my guiding star. Today is 'Shabbat Hagadol'. Happy Birthday. Mania Lichtenstein, 15 April 2000

Nechamka was the middle sister and was Bubbie's playmate and best friend. Only a little more than two years apart, the two of them were always together and Bubbie could not recall them ever fighting.

She described Nechamka as a good soul and always completely selfless; the more quiet, introverted, and serious of the pair, with a round face and curly hair.

Nechamka was an avid reader and smart in school, and taught Bubbie more advanced subjects, such as conjugating verbs in Latin and English, and tutoring Bubbie ahead of her entry exams for gymnasium.

Nechamka had just completed her studies at the gymnasium when the Germans attacked their hometown in 1941.

June 5th was Nechamka's birthday. Her name in Hebrew means *you give your heart / being good*. Bubbie called her 'Chamka' and referred to her as "an angel above my head—always taking care of me."

3

NECHAMKA

My sister – My playmate

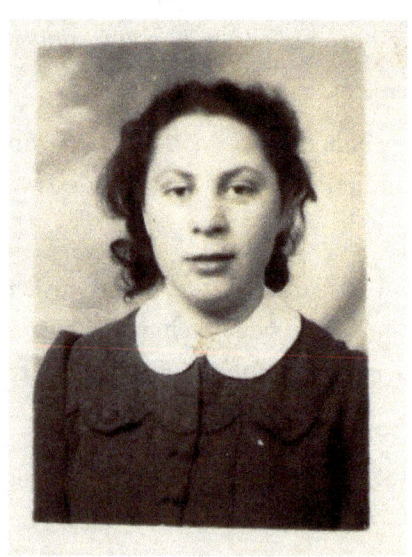

Nechamka

Today is the 19th day of Elul, and the flickering light in the 'Yahrzeit' glass is stirring up many memories. This Yahrzeit is for my entire family, as well as for the 19,000 who were slaughtered on that day. For some reason today, I mainly think of you Nechamka, my sister, my playmate.

My thoughts are taking me back to our childhood and how well we played together. You were only two-and-a-half years older than I, and you had me always trailing after you.

One of our favorite places to play was our outdoor shed. A huge, wooden structure where all kinds of things were stored. What most vividly comes to mind is my custom-made sled, my proudest possession. Mounted high on the shed's wall, patiently waiting for winter, to offer us fun galore. How swiftly this sled took you and me down every hill in the neighborhood. What my sled was to me, to you it was your little ball in a multi-colored net. You would not take a picture without it.

According to today's standards, we had very little, yet we thought we had a lot. We were happy and were never bored. The other objects in that shed, which come to my mind, are our father's tools for tending our garden. It was his cherished hobby.

How rewarding it was, when the garden came to life, and all was in bloom, the three cherry trees were covered with pink blossom, and the golden faces of the sunflowers, tall and bright, seemed like sentinels, guarding the place. To this day, even a picture of a sunflower, brings a tear to my eyes.

Childhood... I sometimes try to bring it back in my thoughts. Today I think a lot of you, Nechamka, my playmate. How nice it would have been having you all these years. But at 22 you were gone among all the others. May you all rest in peace. - Mania Lichtenstein, 1999

Funny Moments

On the 19th day of Elul was the 61st Yahrzeit for my family. Usually it is a day of sad feelings and the past somehow becomes more vivid than the present. Although not in a happy state of mind, I smiled remembering certain incidents.

Nechamka was about six or seven and I four or five years old. On a scorching July day our mother sent us to buy butter. The butter was given to us without as much as a brown bag protection. Well, we sure took our time returning home. We laughed and played all the way until we realized the butter was gone. We licked it to prevent it from running all over us. But to no avail, our hair, faces, and clothes were saturated in butter.

Meekly, we returned home expecting the worst. There was no punishment — what a relief that was! Evidently, the picture we presented was hilarious. There was much laughter and no chance for anger.

Another tragi-comedy that brought a smile to my face took place one summer day. We must have been about five and seven years old. Our summer vacation days were mostly spent at our beautiful river. We picnicked on the luscious grass under old trees, and we waded in the shoal of the river.

One day, it must have been a Friday for our refreshments that day were onion rolls, freshly baked by our mother the night before, Nechamka had an accident. Although we played in the shallow end, Nechamka slipped and began to drown. She was pulled from the water. There was such commotion. She was obviously very scared hollering spasmodically.

While still sobbing she pulled out an onion roll — vigorously biting on it. Her face and the onion roll were soaked in tears. In spite of the trauma that scene looked very funny to me. Poor thing, I never stopped teasing her about it.

Now in retrospect, I realize what a gentle and kind soul she was. I don't remember her ever fighting with me. She always took care of her little spoiled sister. Sweet, kind, Nechamka... gone at 22 years of age. - Mania Lichtenstein, September 24, 2003

4
FAMILY

Gitel, Bubbie, Rivka, Nechamka, and Gershon.

Bubbie had a brother who died at the tender age of five, before Bubbie was born. His name was Meyer. It was later learned that Meyer died of a twisted, infarcted bowel.

When he passed away, the Kaddish — commonly known as a mourner's prayer — was especially important due to the fact Meyer was a boy.

The roots of son-preference lie deep within many cultures, including Judaism, which has long held boys to be more valuable than girls. Fortunately, this has changed in modern times, but at the time of Meyer's death, this was still the case for his family.

Meyer and Rivka, 1918.

Bubbie had no recollection of her maternal grandmother, but she knew her paternal grandmother, Henie Felge, well. Henie lived with her son, Bubbie's uncle.

Bubbie remembered her grandmother as being a proper lady who always kept to herself quietly in the corner of her bedroom. My grandmother never heard her be argumentative or get mad. She was blind, the cause of which was never known. Bubbie, too, had gone blind in her advanced age, which in her case we knew to be from acute macular degeneration.

This disease is considered hereditary and was quite likely the cause of Henie's blindness as well.

Henie Felge

Once a month, Bubbie took her grandmother for a ritual Jewish bath called a *mikvah*. Jewish law requires that one immerses in a mikvah as part of the process of conversion to Judaism.

It is also required of women before getting married and when observing the laws regarding menstrual purity.

A mikvah consists of a pool of water, often some of it from a spring or groundwater wells, in which observant married Jewish women are required to bathe themselves monthly, specifically seven days after their menstrual cycle ended.

It was Bubbie's job because she was the youngest and had the most time to do it. She felt good knowing that she was able to be of some assistance to her grandmother. This ritual cemented their bond. Henie Felge died at the age of 72 in the Holocaust.

My Maternal Grandmother

Her name was Henie Felge. The memory of her brings on pain and nostalgia. I revered, respected, and loved that blind, quiet lady. She lived with her son, his wife, and two children. Although I never witnessed any altercations or disagreements, such a situation, I imagine, could be very tense.

The house was small and simple. She knew to stay out of everyone's way, being such a wise and proper lady. Her bed stood in a corner of the room and she kept to herself mostly to that area. As a young child, I often came to their house to play with my cousin Rozele. She was two years younger than I. A quiet and frail child; she perished like everybody else. My heart breaks when I think of her.

I was not aware how little my grandmother could see, but she always recognized when I was entering. She liked me, and my coming over made her happy. Quite often we played our usual game.

I would ask, "Bubbie, how old are your shoes?" Hesitating a second, as if counting the years, she would reply, "twenty years old!" Then, I asked how old her sweater was and she said, "fourteen years," and so it went on with every item she had on. Being a small child, such number of years seemed inconceivable.

I still recall those nice looking beige shoes and beige cardigan. She was very neat, and her clothes seemed like new. I wish I knew more about her. Nobody who could tell me was spared. All I know is what I perceived through my childhood's eyes.

In her small dark world, she seemed to have managed well, except when she needed to be taken to a doctor, the mikva, and Friday evenings for dinner to our house. That was my duty.

It felt so good knowing I was of some help to her. Now that my eyesight is almost gone, I relate to her even more, and imagine how she must have felt. Having no material things to offer, she gave to us children lots of love and kindness. I will always revere her memory.

At age seventy-two she and my entire family were cleansed from Hitler's world.

Bubbie, I loved you and still do! - Mania Lichtenstein, March 2, 2004

Bubbie's paternal grandparents lived in another city called Lutsk. Once a year, Bubbie would be awakened at dawn by her father so they could catch the train (such a novelty then) to go visit his parents. She referred to these trips as "the biggest excitement imaginable."

She never understood why her father only took her and not her sisters, but as she said, she "will never know." Her paternal grandparents also perished at the hands of the Nazis.

5

LIFE IN POLAND

Bubbie described her hometown, Włodzimierz, as a medium-sized city that was quite cultural for its time because it contained movie theaters, dance halls, and live theater. Her description reminded me of a *shtetl* which is a small town consisting mostly of Jews. Shtetl is a Yiddish word meaning 'town' and "refers to the small pre-WWII towns in Eastern Europe with a significant Yiddish-speaking Jewish population."[1]

Włodzimierz had two gymnasiums, seven elementary schools, and a new agricultural school, which mostly boys attended. Most people kept to their kind. Consequently, only Jews lived in Bubbie's neighborhood and were the majority — at about 26,000 — in the city.

Although Jews were not allowed to own land or property before Bubbie's time, they slowly began settling and multiplying, with numbers that could not be stopped by the Poles. They began establishing stores and homes. And they settled wherever they were permitted, since what they considered their homeland of Israel —

as a state, territory, or even a piece of land — had not yet been born and existed only as a dream, as a homeland to return to.

It's important to note that the very last words of the traditional Passover Seder are "next year in Jerusalem." This phrase, which concludes the Seder, is emotionally significant and important in that it serves as a reminder of past and present suffering and of hopes for freedom in the future. In the past, and prior to World War II, saying "next year in Jerusalem" was just an idea for Jews to have a home to be able to return to. When Israel was created, it became a real possibility.

Money was not spent freely, and people mostly inherited their homes. Hence, migration away from Poland was minimal. The majority of people worked vocational jobs based on skills they developed, as opposed to professional jobs that required advanced education. There were many jobs that Jews performed, including shoe repair, tailor, baker, etc.

Bubbie recalled the early part of her childhood as being very good overall. Although Jews were not treated as equals and anti-Semitism was commonplace, she and her friends did not complain. Instead, they kept to themselves and avoided conflict as much as possible.

Jewish girls went to one school, Christian girls to another; similarly, Jewish boys attended one school and Christian boys another. In the elementary school Bubbie attended, a fence divided the Jewish girls' school from that of the Christian boys. She recalled Christian boys spitting at them, throwing soda cans at them, and calling them names. The girls did not tell anyone in charge, because it would have done no good. Sadly, this kind of behavior was culturally accepted and permitted.

Bubbie told me that other kids would throw stones at her and her friends. She described Polish neighborhood kids as "not kind and very intimidating." As much as possible, the Jewish children were enured to this verbal and physical abuse and would do whatever possible to avoid the harassment.

The girls' school Bubbie attended (2001)

Bubbie spent her days playing with her friends. They were all very poor, and so they would spend time at each other's homes or playing outside when the weather was nice. Her own family enjoyed reading and had a series of books that Bubbie described to me as similar to today's *Little Golden Books*.

During the winter, they skated outdoors. She and her neighborhood friends would use a piece of cardboard to create a makeshift sled and take turns sliding down the snow-covered hills. She recalled one evening when her father brought her to an acquaintance of the family who had made a toboggan just for her.

All summer, Bubbie would wait impatiently for winter to return just so she could use her specially-made toboggan. Everyone envied that sled as they slid down the hills on their pieces of cardboard.

Nearly every day in the summer months, during their one- to two-month vacation from school, they would visit a beautiful river nearby. On Fridays, they would take lunches that usually consisted of onion rolls and other foods her mother had baked the night before.

Bubbie's family had very little extra money, so they did not take many trips, needing to save funds for other more important expenses. More importantly, they found comfort in where they lived and chose not to chance their peacefulness by traveling.

Since money was perpetually tight, children mostly played with rather simple toys like balls. Any toys they owned were valuable to them. Bubbie remembered Nechamka receiving a new toy one year that consisted of a little white bouncy ball and a net. She also recalled this toy being included in a family portrait. It was something of which Nechamka was so proud, and she took great pains to keep it safe.

They also created games to entertain themselves. Bubbie often played an 'intelligence' game with her sisters where they would choose the longest Polish word they could think of, and then compete to see who could come up with the most words derived from it.

Bubbie never owned a store-bought doll but simply made dolls out of kitchen towels. This was something she did for my sisters and me when we were little girls. She also made dolls out of our baby blankets.

Despite what we might consider austere, Bubbie thought her childhood home was very nice, especially when compared to other homes in her neighborhood.

Her house had a kitchen, a study, several bedrooms (she could not recall how many), a den with a desk and green light, and a salon that was used for special occasions and was mostly off limits to the children. Homework was done in the room with the desk with the green light on it. She shared a room with Nechamka and slept in a short, wide bed made of wrought iron. She once banged her head on the bed frame while jumping on the bed, resulting in a permanent scar on her forehead.

The Jewish community had a movie theatre, located on Farna Street, where Bubbie saw some Hollywood movies. Traveling Jewish artists and theatre troupes would visit and put on shows at the theatre as well. Bubbie thought the performances were good but remembers that her mother especially enjoyed them and never missed one.

After dinner, the women would dress up in high heels and hats, and parade down the street to show off their outfits and to see what other people were wearing. Her sisters weren't interested, but Bubbie always went along with her mother.

Sometimes famous singers would come in from places like Warsaw and sing Jewish songs, like 'Tum Balalaika.' My mother learned this song from Bubbie and later she sang it to me when I was young.

There was only one synagogue in town. Because the synagogue was located far from many Jewish homes, the community had a network of houses and boarding rooms throughout the city open to visitors. This was necessary so that Jews could attend the religious service if one needed to pray frequently, such as saying Yitzkor.[2]

The synagogue, considered the heart of her town, was led by Rabbi Yaakov David Morgenstern, thought of as a leader in the community. My grandmother's friend, Genia Seifert, said she believes the synagogue survived the war but wasn't certain.

Perhaps what made Bubbie smile the most was describing the beautiful garden next to her house where her family grew sunflowers, sweet corn, baby cucumbers, radishes, shallots, and green onions, in addition to cherry and apple trees. They also had flowers unique to her native land called 'goźolziki' in Polish, planted at the windows, which carried a perfumed scent, as well as having colorful and bright carnations.

There was also a park in the community. The trees were old, big, and beautiful. There were benches to sit on and paths to walk on. All major celebrations occurred in the park and Bubbie and her friends spent a lot of free time there.

Włodzimierz, picture taken in 2001.

Each year, on November 11, the children went with their school to visit the monument of an unknown soldier. My grandmother recalled official buildings surrounding the outside of the park, but there were also huge areas filled with grass and flowers that she loved to look at.

Our Magic Garden

*There once was a magic spot,
through my childish eyes, most ideal,
where the early spring's warm sun,
on my face I still can feel.
Never a very sound sleeper,
I was up with the tweeting of the birds,
their rhapsodic loud sound had told me,*

that they too were glad to be there.
I still can smell the aroma
that exuded from the rainbow of colors,
I watched it like a mother and baby,
from the first spurts to full grown flowers.
That magic spot was our garden,
that Eden I'll never forget,
and never, never shall I see it again
except through the eyes of my mind.

Mania Lichtenstein, first of March 2000

Bubbie's mother kept a kosher home, but her father did not strictly observe the kosher rules outside the home. They also observed all the Jewish holidays.

Every Shabbat, her mother prepared traditional Jewish foods, such as gefilte fish and challah. Bubbie remembered celebrating Passover (*Pesach* in Hebrew) with her family every spring. Passover begins with the traditional Seder, a ritual feast where the participants tell the story of the Israelites being freed from slavery in ancient Egypt. It can take many hours for the entire story to be told using the Haggadah, a Jewish textbook that explains the order of the Passover Seder.

Bubbie recalled her family discussing the Bible and the Ten Commandments. Rivka led many discussions at the Seder because she had much knowledge to share with her family and Bubbie, being the youngest child at the Seder, asked the traditional Four Questions in either the Hebrew chant or in Yiddish.

Bubbie enjoyed many of the Jewish holidays; she loved celebrating Purim because she was able to dress up in costumes, act out the biblical story in plays, make noise all around the Temple with the grogger, a special noise maker used during the holiday of Purim, and simply have fun.

Sukkot was another holiday that brought many joyous memories. This was a time when she got to enjoy the beautiful outdoors in the fall. While not every family built a Sukkah (a temporary shelter covered in natural materials, built near a synagogue or house and used especially for meals during the Jewish festival of Sukkot) in their yard, Bubbie's neighbors did so every year. Her family was able to eat supper in it with them under the stars.

During Sukkot, families share a variety of foods, such as chicken noodle soup, gefilte fish, and a sweet carrot dish. The High Holidays — Rosh Hashanah and Yom Kippur — were the most strictly observed. Bubbie's parents always went to temple to pray. Gershon belonged to an organization through his medical connections, called the 'Society for health care' and so the family spent the High Holidays with this group every year. On Yom Kippur, everyone is to fast for the full day. Bubbie could only last until lunchtime as a child.

My grandmother was born and raised in Poland until 1939 when the Russians occupied her part of Poland. From 1939-1941, she went to a Russian middle school and all of her studies were changed to Russian. At school, she took classes in arithmetic, Jewish religion, Latin, history, and writing. She was a member of the choir and also participated in music and art. Her teacher taught perspective and how to create depth while drawing trees on a piece of paper.

Bubbie described her childhood life as typical as that of any other child. She ate, slept, attended school and played with her sisters and other children in the neighborhood. She sang songs in Polish and Yiddish at school. When asked what kinds of things she dreamt about, she answered, "I couldn't afford to dream or dream about lofty things." This, she said, was because they did not have the financial means to purchase anything that wasn't strictly necessary. For example, she wanted to learn how to play the piano, but knew this wasn't a realistic dream as her family could not afford to buy a piano.

Although she had a very simple family home, with great delight Bubbie described the one memorable luxury item they owned — a radio made by the German firm Telefunken. This radio, still considered a miraculous invention at the time, allowed them to access other parts of the world. Being a musical family, the radio was a source of immense pleasure.

The family looked forward to every Wednesday evening when the Bulgarian transmission from 'Cafe Paradis' came on and all the beautiful songs and popular hits were played. The next day at school, Bubbie would teach the other children the songs she'd learned the night before. At home, they played a lot of games and engaged in a lot of singing, too. They sang in Polish, Russian, and Yiddish, and Bubbie knew all the popular songs, mainly from listening to them on the radio.

As I mentioned earlier, as a young child, Bubbie often experienced anti-Semitism. She and her friends were frequently called derogatory names. However, Hitler's initial rise to power in 1933 did not affect Bubbie. In fact, she was not aware about the world and politics at such a young age because she "had more important things to do."

But her parents and other adults soon started to realize what was beginning to happen all around them. In 1938, everyone in the neighborhood gathered under the window of Bubbie's home as they listened to Hitler exclaim on the radio, "The Juden, the Juden, the Juden!" just as the boys in his Hitler Youth group would do.

Rivka became aware of many boys at the gymnasium who joined an anti-Semitic organization. In hindsight and with benefit of research, we are now aware the boys were part of the Hitler Youth, which was obvious from the attachment of a pin with a Nazi swastika on their lapel. They would show off the pin to the Jewish kids to express their hatred toward them.

In his book *Mein Kampf*, written in the 1920s, Hitler wrote, "Whoever has the youth has the future." Even before they came to power in 1933, Nazi leaders had begun to organize groups that would train young people according to Nazi principles.

By 1936, all 'Aryan' children in Germany over the age of ten were required to join a Nazi youth group. At ten, boys were initiated into the *Jungvolk* (Young People), and at fourteen they were promoted to the Hitler Youth. Their sisters joined the *Jungmädel* (Young Girls) and were later promoted to the League of German Girls. Hitler hoped that "These young people will learn nothing else but how to think German and act German... And they will never be free again, not in their whole lives."[3]

Although membership of the Hitler Youth organizations was required, many young people were eager and enthusiastic to join, due to the sense of belonging and the importance they felt as members of these groups.

The Hitler Youth was disbanded after the war. However, it is still considered one of the most shocking and chilling facets of the Nazi regime, "proof that a totalitarian state can use children to feed its armies and further its hateful ideologies."[4]

At Christmas time, Bubbie, Rivka, and their mother attended a show at Rivka's gymnasium. In the show there was a scene where a Christian student bullied a Jewish girl by playing a trick on her. He gave the Jewish girl a hoax gift that contained several boxes of decreasing size placed one inside the other similar to a Russian Matryoshka doll and the smallest box contained an onion. This was purely done to mock her and other Jews at the school, and to express their hatred toward all Jews. Although she'd been exposed to anti-Semitism before, Bubbie was surprised by their endless efforts to denigrate and disparage the Jews.

The first real signs of danger that Bubbie experienced from the Nazis were derogatory statements on the radio, as well as from strangers on the streets. They would spew hateful commands exclaiming, "Jews, go to Palestine! Jews, go to Palestine!"

They wanted the Jews to leave their hometown. She then heard rumors that the Poles, who at that time had authority in her city, were gathering Jews and sending them to Madagascar or Africa. My grandmother viewed Madagascar as this "strange, fun place." Her family knew it was in Africa and was, in her mind, probably wild and savage. Still, they thought maybe it would likely be better there than where they were currently living.

Regardless, her family made no attempt to leave the country nor did anyone else they knew. It was not that they wanted to stay, but they did not have any other place to go. Besides, they had little money, and more importantly, this was *their* place, *their* home.

Keep in mind, the world appeared much larger and more intimidating back then than it does today. There were some organizations that helped Jews emigrate to Palestine, now known as Israel, but her family did not try to transfer any assets out of the country or leave, as their small community was the only world they knew.

Her parents, as well as many other Jews, buried treasures, such as rings and other jewelry, when the Nazis began to occupy their country and communities. Bubbie remembered a little gold ring with a red stone she once had that was buried, but she did not know where her parents hid it.

Additionally, she told me that no one believed the Nazi regime would be so bad. They were in complete denial that the Nazis would actually set out to wipe an entire group of people off the face of the planet.

It wasn't long before the war was all around them. Planes were dropping bombs. Anyone even slightly connected to the medical field was given a pamphlet describing all poisonous gases and told to memorize it.

As a pharmacist, Bubbie's father was given one of these pamphlets, and Bubbie thought of herself as his instructor and helped him study it and quizzed him on the material. She felt her father was really proud of her as she had also learned all the numerous kinds of gases, not realizing what they could really do to them. My grandmother had not yet lived through a war and she secretly found this exciting.

6

RUSSIAN CONTROL

In the summer of 1939, Germans on motorcycles invaded Bubbie's hometown.[1] The occupation had begun. Bubbie recalled seeing young, blond-haired Germans entering her town and then heard the first bomb fall. Bubbie and the other children were curious about all the commotion. The adults, however, were extremely worried and understandably frightened.

The Nazis effectively used propaganda to win the support of millions of Germans in a democracy and, later in a dictatorship, to facilitate persecution, war, and ultimately genocide.[2] They were skilled propagandists who used sophisticated advertising techniques and the most current technology of the time to spread their messages.

Once in power, Adolf Hitler created the Ministry of Public Enlightenment and Propaganda to shape the German public opinion and behavior. The Nazi propaganda played an integral role in advancing the persecution and ultimately the destruction of Europe's Jews. It incited hatred and fostered a climate of indifference to their fate.[3] My Bubbie told me that she remembered hearing one German being surprised after talking to a Jew, as his impression was that they were, in his words, "normal people."

Another bomb was dropped, and one of Bubbie's best friends along with her friend's younger sister and father were all killed at once.[4] My grandmother was devastated.

The city was in shambles with glass pieces everywhere and the power lines were down all over the streets. After three days of occupation and bombing, Hitler made an agreement with Stalin to divide Poland in half. His plan was to occupy everything as Napoleon had once done. Hitler figured that he could make peace with Stalin by giving him the eastern side of Poland, and occupy the western part himself.

Bubbie and her family were under the control of the Russian occupation. For Bubbie, life went back to normal, but culturally it was different and surprisingly, in some ways, actually better. She went back to school, but to a Russian school, and was now being taught in Russian. Russians loved to dance and play mandolins, and so Bubbie was able to dance and enjoy music. Even though under Russian occupation, at least she was still living in her hometown. She, along with two other girls and three boys, formed a dance group and they performed at all of the celebrations. It was a fun time for my grandmother at her young age, not realizing the trauma the situation presented to her parents.

Under Russian rule, there was no private enterprise. Everything belonged to the country. In other words, they gave people what they wanted them to have and took what they needed. For example, one day they announced that they would hand out sugar, and so there was a long line of people waiting to get sugar.

The Jews, who were from the western side of Poland under German occupation, migrated to her side of Poland because it was safer during those two years under Russian occupation. As a result, her city became very congested. In an effort to reduce the overcrowding, the Russians began sending many Jews on trains to Siberia.

One day during school, the children heard artillery fire and the Germans occupied their territory again for three days before another agreement was made between Russia and Germany.

Bubbie lived in the Ukrainian area, so she remained under Russian occupation. But then the Russians came into the cities and began seizing people's businesses, including the one owned by her father. The Russians did give everyone a little notice, allowing her family the time to salvage some items such as soap, which was considered a luxury item back then, and they brought it home. Throughout this two-year occupation, my grandmother was not aware of anyone that was murdered in her town.

During this time, Rivka got married to a man named Munia Szafir. She became pregnant and lost her baby. They were married for only seven months when the Russians enlisted Munia in the army and with the German attack following shortly, Rivka never saw him again.

Gershon was forced to work in another drugstore in a neighboring city after the Russians confiscated his shop and he was only able to come home on the weekends. For the adults, having their livelihood taken away was more than demeaning. It was devastating.

7

UNFORGETTABLE IMAGES

Repeatedly, images of naked bodies of men, women, and children move before my eyes. Like a herd of animals, being poked and prodded, made to hurry and jump into a bloody abyss. "Schnell", the executioners yelled. That area had to be quickly readied for the next herd of naked bodies facing the mass graves, the size of which the world has never seen before. They jumped. I imagined hearing thousands of voices, moaning, and the crying of mothers and children. I was reliving it all.

How was I to sleep? 19,000 perished in that first pogrom. Among them were my father, my mother, my grandmother, my sisters, cousins, aunts and uncles, the entire neighborhood. Of the remaining 7,000 town's Jews, two months later, 6,000 met the same fate. They repeated the same route leading now to a smaller mass grave to engulf them. Only 1,000 young and able, I among them, were allowed to remain in a small ghetto. We were forced to produce for the Germans: tailors, shoemakers, candle-makers, knitters, etc.

During one of those forced tasks the following incident I remember well. Sensing our mood and depression, Herr Keller, our supervisor, *felt like adding some "salt to injury" proudly proclaimed, "I, myself, shot 8,000 Jews receiving 30 pfennigs per head." It had enriched him nicely.*

We showed no emotion, knowing well that our fate was sealed. Soon all will be over. After one year and one month since the 6,000 perished, the successful 'Judenrein' was accomplished. Only a handful of 26,000 Jews survived. Due to sheer fate. That would be the only explanation. - Mania Lichtenstein, June 14, 2000.

Włodzimierz Captured

On June 22, 1941, the Germans attacked again, and Bubbie's city of Włodzimierz was captured.[1] The Russians had begun to retreat when they saw the war starting. The Germans announced that all Jews must come out of their homes and identify themselves.

They set up posts to register Jews, to collect data, and to immediately keep an inventory of the entire Jewish population. Each Jewish person was registered with their name, address, sex, and age.[2] Bubbie remembered registering with a group of friends and although they were afraid, they giggled when asked if they were married.

The Germans started to build ghettos by enclosing areas of the city with barbed wire. Two ghettos were set up: the 'living ghetto' for skilled workers, and the 'dead ghetto' for unskilled workers.

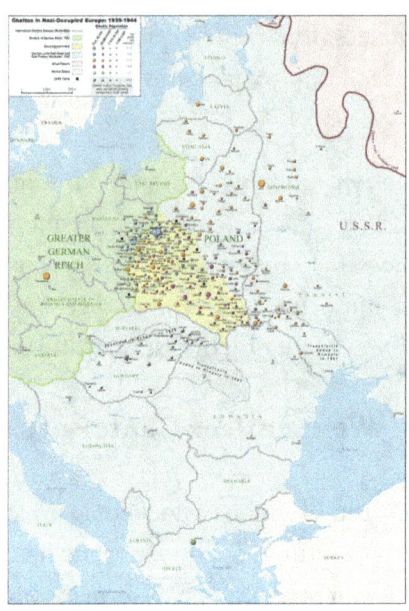

Włodzimierz. Map of the Ghettos in Nazi-occupied Europe 1939-1944. Włodzimierz is located a little north and east of Belzec, a death camp.

Bubbie's house was situated within the living ghetto. She recalled that different families occupied each room of her house — people whom she had not known before. The gates between the two ghettos were guarded by the Jewish police. Passage between them was limited to specific hours.

Her ghetto had a soup kitchen and hospital. The ghetto also contained needlework and shoemaking workshops. Jews were assigned to manufacturing and farm labor. Only those holding work permits could exit the ghetto, leaving and returning daily in groups.

Forced labor camps were created within many ghettos, especially in Poland. According to the U.S. Holocaust Memorial Museum's online encyclopedia, "In the Łódź ghetto, for example, the Nazis opened 96 factories. The ability to work could save one's life, but most often only temporarily."

Jews deemed unproductive by the Nazis were often the first to be shot or deported. Jewish labor, even forced labor, was considered expendable."[3] Forced labor assignments included cleaning for the German police, working in a marmalade factory, delivering mineral water, and agricultural work.[4] My grandmother said that any babies were taken away from their parents, never to be seen again.

Jews were ordered to release all valuable items, such as money, fur coats, jewelry, etc.[5] If anyone disobeyed, they would be shot. Bubbie's family was the only one on the block to have a radio, but had to give it up, along with gold, and Sabbath silver candlesticks.

Money and other valuables that used to be considered precious no longer had significance or meaning to them. All of these precious items had to be given to the Germans. "A degrading scene of robot-like people, bent under the heavy weight of their load, their faces reflecting grief, lined up to deliver as told, items so precious once, and so worthless in the face of death."

Bubbie wrote, "To give up one's candlestick, an inheritance which remained in families for generations and were without fail lit every Friday night, was a distinct sign of destruction of the Jewish home." This is true when for centuries, generations after generations, families light the Sabbath candles every Friday evening. The antique candlesticks I received as a wedding gift, for example, are lit every Friday night that we are all home as a way to welcome in the Sabbath.

Bubbie was especially frightened one afternoon when the Germans stormed into her house and took her mother down to the police station for not turning in her fur coat, which she actually did not own. She said it took agonizing pleading with the Germans to persuade them it was the truth and to let her mother go.

The Jews were now treated like caged animals. They were ordered to make a white band with a *Magen David* (Star of David) to wear on their arm so they could be spotted easily in case they snuck out of the ghettos. This band had to be worn at all times.⁶ They were forced to live in these ghettos for many months.

Each day, hundreds of Jewish men were taken out of the ghetto to dig graves. They were told that two graves were needed. My grandmother somehow learned that the first grave was to be large enough to fit nineteen thousand bodies. Later, a smaller second grave was to be dug for thousands more bodies.

According to survivors I have spoken to, the Nazis did not give the Jews any of this information. However, they learned it through rumors and from Jews who were forced to police the ghettos for the Nazis. The Jewish Police, officially called the Jewish Organization for the Maintenance of Public Order (German: *Jüdischer Ordungsdienst*; Polish: *Żydowska Służba Porządkowa*), comprised of Jewish police units that were established under Nazi occupation in most East European ghettos. "The establishment of a police force usually was connected with the creation of the ghettos, which excluded the Jewish population from general police jurisdiction and thus created a need for an alternative system of ensuring that the Jewish population complied with German occupiers' orders."⁷

The Nazis had a piece of paper stating which ghetto each Jew would be designated to enter. The living ghetto was bigger than the dead one, and it was surrounded by barbed wire. Everyone was trapped inside their ghetto as no one was permitted to leave, unless they were under Nazi supervision in order to perform forced labor.

While every Jew was initially required to wear a white band with a Star of David, the Nazis soon replaced the white armbands with large, five-inch bright orange and yellow patches on the front and back of their clothing so they could be spotted even more easily. The color was so bright that it could be seen from afar.

8

GERMAN OCCUPATION

Bubbie was seventeen years old at the time of the German occupation. Life had changed drastically and suddenly. She sat around with her sisters crying and wishing not to die. The days were long, and so they sang songs to pass the time. When my grandmother was interviewed for the Shoah Foundation Project, she remembered a Polish cabaret song they sang during the many hours at home. She liked it so much because it was a romantic song with a sweet melody.

Food was scarce and everyone remained in a constant state of hunger. In addition, they were very cold as there was no heating. Bubbie and Nechamka sometimes found a momentary escape from the cold by staying in bed under the feather covers, exposing only their eyes waiting for their mother to make her creation of a breakfast potato soup, which was, as a matter of fact, mostly water. At least it was something to eat that could possibly warm them at least momentarily. Her life in the ghettos had acutely changed Bubbie's innocent worldview. She now lived in a constant state of fear.

The Germans mocked and terrorized the Jews on a daily basis, including cutting off their 'payos' which are the sidelocks worn by Orthodox men.

One somber Friday night, they took about one hundred Jewish men, and tortured and murdered them just for the sake of exerting their power and intimidating the other Jews.[1] That night was referred to as 'Black Friday' as it was on Yom Kippur eve, which began on a Friday evening that year. My grandmother said that this event gave them a "foretaste of what was to come. The message became loud and clear."

Bubbie said it was nearly impossible to comprehend the extent of barbarism by the Germans. How could people do such horrors to other people? Everyone had trouble believing how the Germans could actually be fellow human beings. In fact, not everyone wanted to. Some, to the very end, refused to believe the truth of what was happening all around them.

Everybody was starving. There was minimal to no food around as the Germans refused to allow the Jews to eat. They figured it was not worth it to feed people they would soon murder. Commodities once considered important became completely irrelevant. Life was all about how to survive while at the mercy of such horrific and barbaric people. Bubbie, like the others, believed she would be murdered soon, and had to struggle to survive until that fateful moment.

She vividly recalled the long idle days in the ghetto at the beginning. She and Nechamka, perhaps being influenced by their idyllic older sister Rivka were full of romantic dreams that barbed wire could not stop. They dreamt of being young and free, laughing, and promenading on Farna Street, like they used to.

Bubbie said with music flowing through their veins, they would sing while tears rolled down their cheeks. They were young and wanted to live. But this was not normal' and they did not feel like human beings. To help pass the time, they would unravel any old knitted item they could find and would knit it anew. Rivka made a beautiful sweater during this time with an intricate design that Bubbie never forgot. My grandmother said her parents "numbly looked down at us hopelessly."

The Jewish people who lived in the larger living ghetto were useful to the Germans in terms of labor. Therefore, they were kept alive — at least for some time. These Jews had special skills that the Germans needed, such as shoemakers, candle makers, etc. Rivka was able to produce a piece of paper for their father listing him as a bricklayer, although he actually had no skills laying bricks, so they were placed in the living ghetto. Those placed in the dead ghetto knew they were doomed.

The Jews tried to keep track of their holidays while living in the ghettos. They had no communication to the outside world and it was difficult to know what day it was under the lunar calendar.[2] Like any small town, however, there was always somebody who had a calendar and kept track of the days and the holidays. They all tried to observe the Jewish holidays as best they could.

They were quite aware of the slaughtering that was happening all around them and in Eastern Europe at the time, as tales were carried from village to village by someone lucky enough to have survived a massacre.

My grandmother recalled people from neighboring towns sometimes escaped and shared the news of the horrific things they'd witnessed. One boy in particular, from a nearby town, my grandmother knew as he frequented her father's pharmacy, had escaped and warned my grandmother and the others about the slaughtering he saw. Everyone thought he was making up stories and lying. The truth would soon be unmistakable.

In August 1942, the Germans took about 500 women to work in the wheat fields. Their job was to cut the wheat, bundle it, and place the bundles into a machine that would grind the bundles into flour. They were made to work long hours in the blazing sun in the fields. Sometimes there were rainstorms and almost hurricane-like winds, and Bubbie was afraid of the lightning and rain. However, they were not permitted to go to a shelter for safety from these storms.

While working in the fields, the Germans made them all run, not walk. They enforced this by supervising them from horseback and whipping the women with a rope if they were not working fast enough or if they tried to escape. Once Bubbie got whipped in the face by a Nazi because he thought she put too large of a bundle of wheat into the machine. She felt demeaned and insignificant, but she could not afford the luxury of crying as they were just a number to be slaughtered soon.

On the first and second day in the field, they were fed one cup of soup and one small drink of water. On the third day, this stopped. There was no soup or water while working in the hot, open fields. Instead, they had to drink from a frog-infested pond. They were not given any food or water because they believed the Nazis planned to murder them imminently.

Bubbie remembered her grandmother Henie giving her a small sour pickle that she had received from someone else. Although they were all starving and her grandmother could have eaten it herself, she insisted Bubbie take it. This unselfish gesture made Bubbie look at her grandmother as a hero. The pickle was symbolic of her love.

On the third day, they worked until dark. Even during a terrible downpour of rain and through thunder and lightning, they were forced to work. The women were petrified working in such conditions and in an open field. It seemed to my grandmother "even nature was against us." Late at night the trucks finally came to return them to the ghettos. By the way they were treated that day, they knew they did not count anymore.

9

THE BEGINNING OF THE END

After the third day of laboring in the wheat fields, the trucks finally brought us back to one of the two existing ghettos. It was not the one my family lived in. It was late in the evening and I was very anxious to return home. My pleading with the guards at the ghetto gates to let me go home was to no avail. They knew our end was near, why bother...

Given the mood of that night, I could easily sense how very worried my family was. Not returning home meant only one thing to them — I was already dead. How could they endure it? That tragic, sleepless night was witnessed and related to me by a neighbor who survived the first pogrom.

It seemed that everybody could see an invisible sign, announcing our apocalypse. To the contrary of my family's belief, I was not dead, but within hours they were.

What happened there was as follows: when in an unexpected moment the Germans ambushed their ghetto, panic and chaos ensued. The instinct tells one to hide, but where? Those primitive houses had no secret places. The only possible place was the attic.

Normally that place would bring back the fondest memories. As kids the attic was our private haven, where we played for hours. The outside ladder leading to it seemed to have a hundred steps.

In a hurry my father, mother, my oldest sister, Rivka, and my grandmother, who was blind, scaled those steps and entered the attic. At the moment of the ambush, my middle sister, Nechamka, was at a neighbor's house, and had no chance to run back.

All in that house hid somewhere near a stove, from which deadly fumes were escaping, and as a result, all succumbed to asphyxiation. No sooner had the rest of the family entered the attic, their hearts still pounding, when the heavy steps of their hunter's boots were heard ascending the ladder.

The loud barking orders to come out were quickly obeyed. Scared and shaky they were coming down. It was not easy, especially for my grandmother. My father practically had to carry her down.

They were ordered to climb onto cattle trucks already filled to capacity. They knew well their destination. They arrived at the ready mass graves, and stripped of their clothes and dignity, they were swallowed by them. I deal much easier with my own horrid experiences, than with theirs. After all I survived, only due to mere fate. Perhaps it was providence... someone had to tell the world about it. I cannot stop reliving their anguish and pain. - Mania Lichtenstein, February 1999

My grandmother talked about the first 'pogrom' taking place on the first of September 1942.[1] Her use of the word *pogrom* was accurate in the context of what she knew at the time in rural Poland. A pogrom is generally considered to be a violent attack against a group based on their ethnic identity, and is mostly used to refer to attacks against Jews in 19th and 20th-century Europe.[2] Others, commenting on the genocide that took place in Włodzimierz have also described the attacks in this way.[3]

While pogroms may have continued being perpetrated by the local population, mass shootings of Jews were committed by the Einsatzgruppen.

The Einsatzgruppen, or Special Deployment Groups, were special SS and police units tasked with securing occupied territories as German armed forces advanced in Eastern Europe. The squads ruthlessly murdered Jews and political opponents.[4]

Many believe that the systematic killing of Jews in the occupied Soviet Union by Einsatzgruppen and the Order Police (Ordnungspolizei) battalions was the first step of the Final Solution, the Nazi program to murder all European Jews.[5] "In contrast to the methods later instituted of deporting Jews from their own towns and cities or from ghetto settings to concentration camps, the Einsatzgruppen came directly to the Jewish home communities and massacred them there."[6]

This was accomplished by primitive methods of forcing Jews to dig large pits in their hometowns, and then shooting or throwing men, women, and children into them and burying them.

The Einsatzgruppen moved quickly, surprising the Jewish population and leaving them paralyzed and unable to defend themselves.[7] The mass exterminations were well organized and as soon as an area was invaded, the Einsatzgruppen rounded up Jews, Communist Party officials, Gypsies, and members of the Intelligentsia.

If the order called for 'total extermination,' Jewish women and children were included in the roundup. Those rounded up were marched to the outskirts of the city and shot. Their bodies were buried in mass graves, bodies being piled on layer by layer.[8]

At the Nuremberg trial of war criminals in 1946, one of the Einsatzgruppen commanders described a typical massacre:

"The [Einsatz] unit would enter a village or town and order the prominent Jewish citizens to call together all Jews for the purpose of 'resettlement.' They were requested to hand over their valuables and shortly before execution to surrender their outer clothing. They were transported to the place of executions, usually an antitank ditch, in trucks, always only as many as could be executed immediately... Then they were shot, kneeling or standing... and the corpses thrown into the ditch."[9]

(Source of maps: Einsatzgruppen – Animated Map / The Holocaust Encyclopedia)

This was similar to what occurred at Babi Yar, located on the outskirts of Kiev, not far from my grandmother's hometown. On September 19, 1941, the Wehrmacht captured Kiev, Ukraine. Within a week, a number of buildings occupied by the German military were blown up by the Soviet secret police and, in retaliation, the Germans proceeded to kill all the Jews of Kiev.

An order was posted throughout the city in both Russian and Ukrainian:

Kikes of the city of Kiev and vicinity! On Monday, September 29, you are to appear by 7 a.m. with your possessions, money, documents, valuables and warm clothing at Dorogozhitshaya Street, next to the Jewish cemetery. Failure to appear is punishable by death.

From the cemetery, the Jews were marched to Babi Yar, a ravine only two miles from the center of the city. A truck driver at the scene described what he saw:

"I watched what happened when the Jews — men, women and children — arrived. The Ukrainians led them past a number of different places where one after another they had to remove their luggage, then their coats, shoes, and over garments and also underwear. They had to leave their valuables in a designated place. There was a special pile for each article of clothing. It all happened very quickly... I don't think it was even a minute from the time each Jew took off his coat before he was standing there completely naked....

"Once undressed, the Jews were led into the ravine which was about 150 meters long and 30 meters wide and a good 15 meters deep... When they reached the bottom of the ravine they were seized by members of the Schutzpolizei and made to lie down on top of Jews who had already been shot. That all happened very quickly. The corpses were literally in layers. A police marksman came along and shot each Jew in the neck with a submachine gun... I saw this marksman stand on layers of corpses and shoot one after the other... The marksman would walk across the bodies of the executed Jews to the next Jew who had meanwhile lain down and shoot him."

Over the next week, 33,771 Jews were murdered at Babi Yar. The following months, Babi Yar remained active as an execution site for Gypsies and Soviet prisoners of war.

Soviet accounts after the war estimate 100,000 killed and while different research cites and articles do not substantiate that number, the true number of those assassinated will likely never be known.[10]

In listening to the details of the way my grandmother described each of the pogroms she experienced, I am able to further benefit from the research conducted in the late 20th century.

I am quite confident that the highly organized, disciplined, weaponized paramilitary force was early evidence of the Nazi's goal to literally exterminate all Jews from the face of the earth, the Final Solution,[11] which is exactly what the Einsatzgruppen were commissioned to do.

These acts were not the same as those my grandmother and her town experienced as anti-Semitism, or harassment but instead catastrophic genocide. For the sake of using consistent words that mirror what my grandmother wrote about and described in her poems and prose, I will continue with the use of the word 'pogrom.'

My grandmother recalled that at 11 p.m. on the first of September 1942, which was on the third day of her working in the wheat fields, she and everyone else there were packed tightly like cattle into three trucks and driven back to the dead ghetto. When Bubbie got there, she started crying. She told them that she lived in the other ghetto.

The Ukrainians worked closely with the Nazis. According to the "Operations and Situation Report No. 6 by the Einsatzgruppen of the Security Police and SD in the U.S.S.R. (for the period October 1-31, 1941)" there was great bitter hostility among the Ukrainian population against the Jews because it was thought that the Jews were responsible for the explosions in Kiev. They were also seen as informers and agents, who unleashed the terror against the Ukrainian people.

All Jews were arrested in retaliation for the arson in Kiev, and altogether 33,771 Jews were executed on September 29th and 30th, 1941. "Gold, valuables and clothing were collected and put at the disposal of the National-Socialist Welfare Association (NSV), for the equipment of the Volksdeutsche, and part given to the appointed city administration for distribution to the needy population."[12]

So when the Ukrainians brought everyone from the wheat fields to the dead ghetto, and my grandmother started to cry and plead with them to take her to the living ghetto, they laughed at her and would not let her return to her family.

My grandmother was the only one of her family to be working in the wheat fields and she feared that her mother would already believe that she had been killed.

When she arrived at the dead ghetto, it was close to midnight. Rivka's in-laws lived there, and so she sought them out that night. Bubbie found her sister's cousin (by marriage) named Popa, who was only fourteen years old, Popa's mother, and her two siblings — a six-months-old and a four-year-old.

They stayed up all night and remained fully dressed in case something was to happen suddenly. Nobody talked all night and it was 'dead quiet' because they all knew they were about to be killed. Nobody stirred, nobody slept. According to Bubbie, that night was a very long night as they all knew what their fate would soon be.

At dawn, they could see they were surrounded by Germans and Ukrainians with automatic rifles in their hands and ready to strike. They knew "this is it."

At 6 a.m. on the first of September 1942, the Germans entered the dead ghetto.[13] The first shots were heard and everyone screamed, kicked, and there was absolute chaos. Bubbie, her sister's in-laws, and some extended relatives ran to a hiding place. They could hear the German boots stomping and looking for their prey. A prominent family they knew lived on the third floor. Bubbie, Popa, and the extended family all followed this family who lived there.

The back wall contained an armoire and the back of the armoire slid open and behind that was a door to a secret attic where they could hide. Down below, she heard Popa's mother moaning as she was led out with her two little children. Wherever there was a baby, the hiding place would be exposed. Bubbie heard Popa's mother screaming and felt completely helpless. Everybody was desperate to survive and nobody could hide a crying baby from the Nazis.

She and the others hid in the attic for fifteen days. It was extremely hot and they all sat crouched, mute, motionless, and listened somberly to all of the horror outside. They could hear the Germans tearing apart every Jewish house, looking for anyone hiding anywhere. Because 19,000 Jews were supposed to perish, they could hear them stomping on roofs searching for more Jews. Bubbie and the others stayed in the dark attic without food or water. Through the blinds they could see what was going on in the other ghetto.

Great panic ensued when the Germans set ablaze the living ghetto and they were all smoked out.[14] In the living ghetto, the people were packed like dead sardines and brought to their grave.[15] 19,000 were buried together.

Bubbie recalled that the Germans kept telling them not to worry because they were in the living ghetto, but all of this was a lie and done to keep them calm. The people were hysterically crying and reciting a prayer called the 'Shema.'

Shema Yisrael ("Hear, O Israel") are the first two words of a section of the Torah that is the centerpiece of the morning and evening prayer services, encapsulating the monotheistic essence of Judaism: "Hear, O Israel: G-d is our L-rd, G-d is one."

Its recitation twice daily (morning and evening) is a biblical commandment. In addition, it is recited just before retiring for the night, as well as in the Kedushah service on Shabbat. The prayer has become so central to the Jewish people that it is the climax of the final Ne'ilah prayer of Yom Kippur, and is traditionally a Jew's last words on earth.[16]

By 1 p.m. they were all taken on the trucks, past the living ghetto, and towards a place called Piatydnie, where the massive two graves were awaiting them.[17]

According to Yad Vashem, the Germans killed 15,000 Jews from the city of Włodzimierz near the village of Piatydnie, twelve kilometers west of the city, on September 1-3, 1942.[18] The living ghetto was an inferno. This was the day Bubbie's family and the living ghetto were murdered.

The Silence I Hear

I hear you well my dear ones,
Through the utter silence from afar,
Past miles of ocean well hidden,
Forgotten by the world by now.
Once only I saw that place of horror,
Adorned on one side with lush pine forests,
On the other a vast endless field,
Where all you silenced forever now rest.
Two mass graves hiding twenty-five thousand,
Jewish corpses of young and old,
Could it be a silence that resonates,
Or cries of anguish I hear?

At least by now you suffer no more,
The dark, bloody days are gone,
I'll remember forever your moans and tears,
And the eternal silence I'll hear.
The horrid site in a remote corner in Poland,
Is called 'Piatydnie.'
The year was 1942.

Mania Lichtenstein, September 2002

10

LIFE IN THE ATTIC

My grandmother told me that somehow, because of "fate," their roof was not torn apart, and she, and the others, remained alive. The courageous family whose house they were hiding in brought them a bag of biscuits to share. There was also a sack of peas, a raw potato, and a few pieces of zwieback, a dry bread. They did not know how long they would be there.

For two days, they barely ate anything aside from a biscuit. There was no water and they were extremely dehydrated. After eight days, a young teenage boy named Plot, who was hiding with them, remembered there was some water on the balcony. He bravely ventured out and returned with some stale, green water that would normally be used for washing hair but not drinking; however, everyone took a sip. Rivka's father-in-law gave the children his sip when it was his turn to drink. It was a noble act and water meant so much more to my grandmother from that day on.

Nobody felt like a human being anymore. They were all very skeletal and very weak. Their clothing was getting big while their bodies were shrinking. Due to lack of strength from starvation and dehydration, they all had to hold onto things to walk and nobody spoke for days. They didn't think about food or surviving.

And in fact, not having food was a blessing in disguise because they wouldn't have to relieve themselves as much, which was embarrassing to do in full view of the others. Bubbie did wonder though why her mother, father, and sisters had been killed and not her.

One day, they heard the Ukrainians on the roofs banging. They were tearing off roofs looking for more Jews. They knew that many Jews were hiding in attics and she could hear them say, "Will we find Jews here?" as if they were digging for gold. Luckily, they did not tear the tin roof off or shoot at it where Bubbie was hiding.

The Ukrainians and Germans were relentless in finding every living Jew. They looked through the spaces in the attic windows or found Jews running and hiding in the streets. They listened and sought to kill more.

Bodies were laid out side by side in layers in the graves. Each layer of bodies was sprayed with bullets and then covered with a new group of bodies. It did not matter to the Nazis if any bodies underneath were still alive.

Bubbie knew a fourteen-year-old girl from her school who was the last one to be shot on a particular day, although she was only hit in the leg. In the middle of the night, while the grave was still uncovered, she regained consciousness and ran from the grave to the nearest house where a farmer lived. He took pity on her and let her hide in his home.

In the afternoon on the fifteenth day, through the cracks in the attic walls, Bubbie and the others saw a group of emaciated and wobbly Jews being led by the Germans. When they were gone, most certainly to face the same fate as the others, the pogrom ended.[1] 19,000 Jews had been killed.[2]

People slowly began emerging from their hiding places. Now that a quota had been met, people were no longer being shot or taken on trains anywhere. My grandmother always described the Germans with words such as, 'precision' and 'organization.' She said they kept meticulous records and were excellent at math and keeping numbers. So, once the quota was met for this first pogrom, not one more person would be killed.

Bubbie said she survived this first pogrom by not being allowed to return home after the long day in the wheat field, and she found herself in the wrong ghetto. She said quite matter-of-factly once again, "It was fate."

She and the others started leaving the attic. They emerged like skeletons, barely able to walk, with no energy, and severe weakness. They were free for the time being and immediately they started roaming. Every house was empty. They looked for anything and anybody.

Bubbie thought it was futile to hope that perhaps someone from her family survived. She checked, but all that she found was emptiness. Popa and her found flour and mixed it with water and baked bread. Bubbie remembered drinking water and then suffering from diarrhea after having gone so long with so little water.

The Germans continued to organize the remaining Jews. A smaller ghetto was created for the remaining 7,000.[3] They opened up a kitchen and gave them some food, like standard procedure, as if nothing terrible had just occurred. Six days after the first pogrom ended a considerable number of surviving Jews ended up succumbing to dehydration.

Rivka's father-in-law died as soon as he lay down after coming out of the attic. There was hardly any elderly person or baby alive. Bubbie knew somebody who knew the name of the German leader in charge of the operation that exterminated so many innocent

Jews. She was told he was a top Ukrainian called "Ivan the Terrible."

The Nazis brought the clothing of the murdered Jews to a school, the 'Red School,' and had the remaining Jews separate the garments.[4] My grandmother was in this forced labor camp, as opposed to a concentration camp. This allowed her to escape being tattooed unlike so many other Jews.

While sorting through the clothing, she saw Rivka's sweater. She knew it was hers because Rivka had knitted it herself in the first ghetto. It was pink and purple and had an intricate design on it involving a square and a line on both sides. Next to it Bubbie saw her grandmother's only pleated jacket. She did not cry when she saw the items as she thought of her family members as the lucky ones. They were now at peace. They were in heaven.

Bubbie's family perished during the first pogrom. Her sister Nechamka, however, was not with her family when she too was killed. When the raid took place, Nechamka was at their cousin Sania's house. In a panic, Sania's father, mother, sister, brother, and Nechamka hid in a hole somewhere near the stove. All of them were asphyxiated.

Bubbie and Sania were both separated from their families. Sania obtained the information of their deaths from someone they knew. He was told where he could find their bodies. The Germans gave them permission to look for their bodies and to dig a hole next to the house to bury them there. The two of them dug for hours, but they were unable to find their bodies. At the age of 21, Nechamka was another statistic among the 19,000 that had been initially killed.

Bubbie was now one of six girls who lived in a cubicle. After two months of living there, the second pogrom began. It took two more pogroms after the first one to eliminate the 26,000 Jews in total living in Bubbie's hometown before the war. 'Judenrein' or *Clean of Jews*, the goal of the Nazis was realized.

11

A NEW GHETTO

But it was not over. Another ghetto area was created, and once again the Nazis separated the Jews into parts known as the 'living ghetto' and the 'dead ghetto.'

My grandmother was assigned to the dead ghetto and recalled that the German leader's last name assigned to her area was something like Westingheider. In this ghetto, Bubbie lived with five other girls in a little cubicle: Popa Fine and Genia Seifert, plus Hanka, Tzipora, and Batia (last names unknown). They had a kitchen where she remembers they drank coffee. She also told me there was no garden and that she no longer sang or dreamed and there was no laughing.

By now, Bubbie had lost all hope of surviving. She went to work every day for the Germans. She told me about one day when she'd somehow cut her eyebrow on a window frame resulting in a significant loss of blood. The Germans permitted her to leave work and go back home to the ghetto to attend to the injury.

Bubbie knew a couple who was assigned to the living ghetto and that night, the woman, Hanka Oks, asked Bubbie to come over as she knew Bubbie was hungry and she'd managed to make a little soup. Since Bubbie was not at work that day, she went over to the couple's ghetto for the night.

In November 1942, two months after the first pogrom, the second pogrom began.[1] One morning, everyone within the 'dead' ghetto was extinguished within a few hours. 8,000 Jews. Murdered. 1,000 Jews, including Bubbie, were left alive in the living ghetto. Bubbie said that had she not spent the night with friends, she would have been captured and killed like some of her roommates. "It was fate," she said again matter-of-factly.

After the second pogrom, the remaining Jews in the living ghetto were moved to even smaller ghettos. Bubbie talked of seeing people running naked through the open graves and being shot at with an automatic rifle. She heard a drunken German boasting that he'd personally shot and killed 10,000 Jews. She thought about her parents and was, in a way only made possible by the horrors she'd witnessed, relieved that they did not survive. She did not think her mother could have coped if she'd survived and her daughters had not. Bubbie said that the German operation was done with soulless precision and intensity.

One of her friends told Bubbie she'd witnessed the Germans murdering her family at the graveside. With such horror and depression, her friend had begged the Nazis to shoot her as well. The Nazis ignored her request for death and ordered her to return to the ghetto. Apparently, they chose not to shoot her because their daily quota of murdered Jews had been reached.

During one of my many discussions with Bubbie about the details of her survival, she made a point to tell me she'd initially thought a total of 26,000 Jews were murdered during the second pogrom. She then remembered Popa correcting her years ago stating that it was actually the total number of 28,000 thousand Jews that had been killed.

It has been documented that between September 1-3 in Włodzimierz, the Einsatzgruppen were responsible for shooting 25,000 Jews from the local area at Piatydnie. On November 13, 1942, the Germans killed another 3,000 Jews from the town near Piatydnie.[2]

The Little Brown Shoe

Far removed from our city, in a deserted place, two mass graves stood silent. They were dug earlier by Jews, many of whom never held a shovel in their hands. But, under the watchful eyes of the Germans, in sweat and exhaustion, the project was completed. One big grave to contain 19,000 bodies and a smaller one for 6,000.

The first pogrom came and 19,000 bodies were ready to fill one grave. Two months later the second pogrom produced 6,000 more. So far, the plan was working. All was quiet. No more will tumultuous wailing, crying, moaning be heard, like when they were jumping into the graves to be shot.

But, something went wrong. The Jewish blood began rebelling. There was not enough space for it, in those crammed graves. It burst loose and a 'red sea' emerged. At that time only a thousand young Jews remained in a small ghetto, kept to be used for cleaning up all dirty jobs, like that one for instance, equipped with shovels, we were ordered to eradicate that spooky site, to cover up and erase any evidence.

They were not worried about us bearing witness, for we too will be silenced in a couple of months.

As I was approaching the graves, my eyes caught a little brown shoe, trampled into the ground by thousands of feet. All clothing of the victims, that were worn a long while ago, were brought back to the ghetto for us to assort, before being sent off to Germany. Only one little brown shoe of a child of three or four was left behind. Perhaps to be a reminder of human atrocities that took place at that forsaken site. The image of that little brown shoe often comes to my mind. I like to call it the 'Little Monument.' The only monument. - Mania Lichtenstein, September 1998

12

ONE THOUSAND REMAINING

With only 1,000 Jews left, another ghetto was created just for people with trades. It appeared the Nazis were only keeping alive those of value to them. In this ghetto, Jews were required to carry a piece of paper with them at all times. If a Jew did not have the requisite piece of paper that listed the person's trade, they remained in hiding. Bubbie did not have such paper.

There was a candle-maker who was living in this ghetto who once knew Bubbie's father. He recalled a favor her father once had done for him before the war. He offered to repay the favor by helping Bubbie. He knew a man named Leon Hirschhorn from Czechoslovakia who had an extra piece of paper. His wife had been shot dead on the street because she had walked outside without her identification paper. The candle-maker gave that piece of paper to Bubbie and she was so grateful to receive it, as it meant life. Without it, she would have eventually been shot as well. The paper described her trade as "work in shop." The woman's year of birth was 1906, and with my grandmother being so frail and childish-looking, she had to erase the 'o' and write in a '1' to better reflect her age. But for now, Bubbie had the all-important *Ausweis* (identification paper) that would eventually help save her life.

This new ghetto was called *Handwerker-Genossenschaft*, which means 'tradesmen cooperative.' It housed about fifteen young women who were forced to work for the German soldiers and their Polish girlfriends in the knitting workshop.

The Germans supplied the wool that the women knitted into hats, mittens, and socks for them. Bubbie said, "Knitting and daydreaming went well together and every daydream we related started with 'If we survive...'" They all thought a lot about food, too. Bubbie said people would say, "If I survive, I'll have a roast beef."

But for my grandmother, she really thought about sweets. She thought that if she survived, she would eat cake and jam. She even jokingly said that as a dowry, should she get married, she would want to receive a large jar of jam, adding, "I'll jump into that jar and I'll dwell in it."

Her favorite meal came from two boys who snuck out a bottle of oil and she and the others found a tomato in the garden. They all ate it together with some salt and the oil the boys brought back. She said it had the most heavenly taste and that she was never again able to taste anything as wonderful for the rest of her life as that single tomato.

It was during this time that Bubbie wanted so much to visit where her childhood home had once stood. At great risk to her life, she did in fact make her way back there. As she'd expected, all was gone except for a pile of bricks, a few broken pots, one of her father's socks, and one of Rivka's beautiful pale blue slippers.

No matter the destruction human beings bring upon themselves, however, Bubbie said, "Nature wants no part of it, and goes on perpetuating its task." She noticed that the Germans could not completely eliminate the spot that was once her beautiful garden, her 'magic dreamland.' The cherry trees her father had tended to for so many years still had their trunks covered with the white paint he had used to protect the trunks from cracking. And the trees were in blossom, as if in pink-white defiance to say that life will go on and on.

Bubbie described life in this ghetto as uneventful, except for some of the 'dirty' jobs they were forced to do, such as clearing debris from a leveled Jewish home. One time, Bubbie was taken with others to a thinly covered mass gravesite where the bodies were beginning to decompose.[1] Blood saturated the soil, attracting wolves and wild dogs. Bubbie and the others were given shovels and told to cover the graves with more mud.

"Every time we dug in," she said, "a head with hair appeared. It could have been our mothers' or sisters'." They existed in a state of numbness in order to endure such gory work.

Bubbie did this for one year, one month, and one day exactly after the second pogrom. And that is precisely when the third pogrom occurred, when the Germans decided to eliminate the remaining 1,000 surviving Jews on a December morning in 1943.[2]

It was early and Bubbie and the others were getting ready for their daily work. Suddenly there was chaos everywhere. The Germans and Ukrainians stormed the ghetto shooting at everything that moved. They had no need to search as all the victims were right there and fell straight into their hands. They gathered up everyone in the ghetto.

People were running all over like scared mice. My grandmother described the scene as looking like "ants on the white snow," as they were running but there was no place to hide and it was impossible to create a hiding place. Bubbie started running, like the others, without knowing where to run.

She and a few others found a little deserted shed, much like one in which people might keep wood, with only little space inside. They all stood inside pressed against each other, unable to move their arms or bodies. Bubbie estimated that there were twenty people packed inside, including Popa, from whom Bubbie had not separated since the first pogrom. They stood inside that shed praying silently for their lives. They stood there motionless all day long without food or water, listening to the horror outside as the soldiers continued searching for anyone to kill. This was the Nazis' last stage of accomplishing their mission.

In the middle of that interminably long night, there was no sound outside. It was as though everything had come to a standstill. The air was so dense inside that little shed that eventually from their own breathing, moisture formed on the ceiling and started raining down on them. It became physically unbearable to continue standing there.

Emotionally, nobody wanted to accept what was happening. They knew they would have to leave the shed or likely die right there. So, it was decided that they would leave. Unanimously, they decided to escape from the shed and take the risk of being killed. They ran out of the shed by two every ten minutes. The ghetto was empty. My grandmother said, "Only the dogs barked like mad." She ran out with Popa.

The ghetto was deserted even by the German guards, and the two of them left through an opening in the wire fence somebody else had made. It was pitch dark and everyone in the town seemed to be asleep.

Janina Zawadzka.

Bubbie did not know where to run or hide. Fortunately, Popa knew a Polish woman named Janina Zawadzka who might be willing to help them.

Prior to the war, this woman had received some valuables from Popa's parents in exchange for a hiding place should the need ever arise. She lived in the outskirts of the city.

At approximately 3 a.m. they ran to her house and knocked on her door. She was a good woman with a big heart. She knew what was happening to the Jews and was very distraught about it.

Janina Zawadzka.

My grandmother said, "She had such pity on us and cried over what was being done to the Jews. She was one of the few Poles who had a heart where the Jews were concerned." Bubbie often described the Germans as wanting to hurt the Jews, but the Poles and Ukrainians she would say, "Would pour salt on the wounds."

However, Janina let them come in and hide under the covers of a little bed in a small room since there was no actual hiding place for them. Her neighbors became suspicious when they noticed she was constantly locking her front door, and they questioned her about whether or not she was hiding any Jews.

Although it was January and bitter cold due to the severe winter, Bubbie and Popa moved to her outdoor stables and hid there with the horses. Bubbie said that while the smell of the horses' urine was so bad, they considered themselves lucky to have found shelter. My grandmother wrote, "I must say that this woman was an angel, her name was Janina Zawadzka, poor and not of best of health, and the little food she had, she was willing to share with us."

Janina, who had entertained German soldiers by feeding them during Christmas (she'd felt bad they had to be away from their families during this time), got progressively more nervous about hiding Bubbie and Popa at her house, and she would pray every day that the Germans would not discover them.

Two months later, when it had finally become too much of a burden for her to take, she came up with a plan to have a peasant she knew take Bubbie and Popa to the woods with his horse and wagon. My grandmother said that Janina told them she was sending them 'to the woods' like in the story of *Hänsel and Gretel*. It was risky, but they had no choice.

Janina gave a Polish partisan peasant, who was stationed nearby and whom she trusted, a bottle of vodka to give to the German guard in exchange for him to allow Bubbie and Popa to pass. He was asked to say, "Hey comrade, here's a bottle of vodka, you must be frozen." And the idea was that the German guard would take the vodka and not have time to inquire as to who the girls were before they passed. It was fate again, as the guard let them pass, and my grandmother said that they "suddenly felt free" and out of the zone of danger.

Bubbie and Popa wrapped themselves in shawls to disguise their Jewish identity and to keep themselves warm and then left for the forest. The road to the woods took several hours, the wagon constantly shaking and sliding on the ice.

13

IN THE FOREST

Despite their new-found sense of freedom, the war was still raging, and they had no radios to inform them as to what was going on. Bubbie and Popa went from house to house asking Poles for help. Bubbie told me that the reason the Poles were tolerant of the Jews was because they were in trouble with the Germans themselves. The Germans, being aware of the partisans' whereabouts, kept attacking them constantly, and the Poles bravely fought back. There was also a lot of friction between the Poles and the Ukrainians, constantly attacking and killing one another. Because of all this, they didn't have time to worry themselves with the Jews.

Bubbie and Popa went door to door looking for work. They once got lucky when a Polish squire hired them to knit all kinds of items for their little son. They slept on a straw floor and were fed adequately with 'real food.'

They stayed there until the Germans came with the airplanes and dropped bombs on the villages, as they were aware of these Polish Partisans. So Bubbie and Popa ran deep into the woods to hide. There were also many peasants who ran into the woods to hide their cattle because they knew the Germans were going to bomb again soon.

Bubbie and Popa met up with a group of young Jews who had escaped from the ghettos earlier. Among them were the brothers Joseph and Moishe Lichtenstein, who were part of the partisan resistance.

Joseph Lichtenstein (1946)

Moishe Lichtenstein (1946)

The Lichtenstein brothers were from Bubbie's hometown and they all knew of each other but not very well. Now, however, they immediately thought of each other as their new 'family' and they kept together as a little group.

As such, they shared everything and traveled east together trying to evade the Germans. If they found a potato, the four of them would share it. They bonded as family because none of them had anybody else, and they were all trying to help each other survive.

In describing this new kinship, my grandmother never once claimed any credit for a good decision. She never used the word 'I' or 'me.' Instead, she always used words like 'we' or 'us' — the four of them were a group, a new family.

For someone who knew six languages well, her choice of words was conscious and deliberate as she was raised to be modest and truly saw, cherished, and valued the new family unit.

From time to time, they would seek shelter and food in exchange for work, and then they would return to the forest. This did not last long as they were almost on the front line and the artillery and bombings were growing frighteningly closer.

After surviving two bombings with casualties, Bubbie, Popa, Joseph, and Moishe continued to stay together as they escaped farther back into the woods desperately trying to put as much distance between the front line and themselves as possible. They knew they'd have to take a risk soon, as they couldn't hide forever in the woods.

They met a Russian dispatcher in the woods who told them where the Russians were stationed and told them that the only way they were going to survive was to run to the Russian side. The partisan group had rifles and allowed the Jews to be near them. They did not actively protect them or want them to be there, however, as they had "more important missions."

Bubbie would tell me that "the sound of war at our footsteps," could be heard wherever they went. Although they didn't have a radio, they continued to glean accurate information from the ever-present rumors.

What they learned was heartening. The Russians were successfully pushing the Germans back west and recapturing city after city. The Germans were "dying like flies," due to the severe cold winter, as they were not well-equipped to deal with the harsh cold. Suffering and disillusionment were breaking the German army's spirit, and defeat was on the brink.

Every time a plane approached, Bubbie and her friends camouflaged themselves and pressed their bodies against a pine tree. One day, my grandmother's shoe soles broke in half, which allowed pine needles and stones to enter her shoe base and injured her foot. Joseph managed to find a rag, which she wrapped around her bleeding foot.

In general, when the Russians met up with them, they knew they were loathed. The Russians would tell them how mad they were at the Jews because of how terrible the war was, and they senselessly blamed the Jews for it.

With luck on their side, they met another Russian military representative in the woods who was kind to them. He told Bubbie and the others where the Russians were stationed, which helped them escape. Bubbie, Popa, Joseph, and Moishe were still in the front line and bombings were expected, and so this information was helpful to them to know which direction to travel in hopes of finding safety.

While still in hiding, Moishe and a few friends decided to steal one horse each with no saddle. While Moishe never rode a horse in his life, he rode it bareback with his friends. The boys were eventually caught by the Russians and thrown in jail. A Russian captain ended up releasing them when he found out they were Jewish as he was, too. He warned the boys that if they ever got caught doing something like this again, they would be hung.

My grandmother wrote this in Polish:

```
1944 (in the forest)

Czy to nie jest tragicznie, przy tak młodych latach, tak opuszczoną
być w życiu,
I czy nie strasznie być samą, samotną, pzechodzić dnie pełne goryczy.
Me dnie upływają jak statki po wodzie, ich sterem jest moja tęsknota,
I upływają tak szybko odemnie, lecz coż pozostaje - Tęsknota..
Z tą samą tęsknotą się budzę i kładę, z grymasem tym samym na ustach,
Z pytaniem tym samym "Gdzie wy jesteście?"
A izba jest pełna, lecz pusta.
A to w dodatku jest wiosna na dworze, jak wszystkie i ta, identyczna,
Jej wietrzyk mnie codzień przebudza, lecz poco ?
Podziwiać jaka ona klasyczna.
O wiosno, nie mogę podziwiać twych wcięków, twoj zapach świerzutki
lecz ostry,
Gdyż co mnie najmilsze, wydarte zostało,
Kochani rodzice i siostry.

MANIA LICHTENSTEIN. 1944
```

1944
In the Forest
(translated)

Isn't it tragic at such a young age
to be left alone in life,
Isn't it terrible to be left alone,
lonely, and to go through my days full of longings.
My days go by like ships in the water,
their steer is my longings,
And moving away from me so fast
and what is left,
it's longings.
With the same longings
I am waking up and going to bed,
with same grimace on my lips,
with same question: Where are you all?
And the room is full,
but it is empty.
In addition, it is spring outside,
like all the others and this one it is identical.
Every day the light wind is waking me up,
but for what?
I admire how classic it is.
Spring, I can't admire your beauty,
And your fresh but sharp smell,
Because everything that was nice to me,
it was taken from me.
My dear parents and sisters.

Mania Lichtenstein

14

LIBERATION

German planes flew low over the woods enabling them to see what was ahead of them on the ground. Bubbie and the others were worried that they would soon be back to eradicate the whole area. They had an urgent need to escape. To do so, they had to cross the front lines where the sounds of artillery never stopped. They split up into small groups and walked sometimes as much as 60 kilometers a day. Based on the information they'd been given by the Russian military representative, they were able to head toward recaptured cities, moving farther away from the front.

In truth, they liberated themselves. It took a few days for them to walk from the forest until they reached a city liberated — and now occupied — by the Russians.[1] They expected to be greeted with awe as if "we came from outer space," Bubbie told me. Instead, they were appalled to discover how cruel and ruthless the Russians were to the Jews. They were not allowed to register in any of the Russian-held regions and were forced to continue migrating from city to city. Regardless, they were free among free people and that sense of freedom was palpable.

The lingering terror and nightmares of the war, however, continued to haunt them. They stayed in empty Jewish houses and ventured out in search of food and water. The freedom felt was very 'mighty,' but it remained blemished because night after night they heard the exploding bombs and saw the sky light up like one ball of fire. Every night when hearing the bombs, they sought refuge in a cellar.

One night a bomb fell onto the building they were staying in, destroying the upper floors, but not the floor where they were staying. Amazingly, they were buried in debris but uninjured. They screamed and called for help, and were eventually dug out. Once again, they had survived.

Due to the relentless hatred, they'd long endured as Jews, they kept on the run, too afraid to stay long in any one place. To exacerbate matters, there were no permitted resources to help Jewish survivors resettle after the Holocaust.

In fact, all they really wanted was to go home. Bubbie had not known how much longer she would have to live, and so the word 'tomorrow' did not exist. Each day she would just "live for the day." She wrote, "It is unbelievable how much one takes for granted: freedom, respect, water, food, and sleep..."

She and the others followed behind as the Russian Army recaptured city after city. Włodzimierz, Wolynski was liberated on July 20, 1944.[2] When they heard their hometown was liberated, they made their way back there. She told me she had not hoped of finding anything in particular but they had nowhere else to go and no purpose in life anymore. They were hoping to maybe find a living relative as they'd heard of others who were finding family members.

Bubbie, however, knew her family had all perished during the first pogrom. None of their neighbors were alive. My grandmother estimated that of the 26,000 people who had lived there, perhaps fifteen to twenty youth survived.

When they arrived in their hometown, they saw the Jewish homes had been destroyed. As they wandered from street to street, they received dirty looks from the Poles. The Poles thought of them as an extinct species and made degrading remarks such as, "How dare you show up again!"

Mania and Joseph (1945).

Still, they remained in their hometown, where Bubbie and Joseph got married on October 15, 1944. A few of their fellow survivors attended their little ceremony. Unfortunately, the Russians heard about the wedding and demanded the vodka and the bride.

All evening, Bubbie remained locked up in a room. The ruthless Russians stormed in and seized the one bottle of vodka. Despite it all, Bubbie and Joseph still got married.

15

MY HOME

So many memories stir in my mind and many escape, until one day they appear again. Unlike my mind, the written words won't ever let the memories escape. Lately I think a lot of our house, the way it was then. I recall every room, the things that were in it, and how my family lived and dreamt in that house.

I am the only one who survived. Three times I felt like being summoned back to that ghostly place. Perhaps to try to resuscitate it by bringing it back to the way it once was. I do not remember how I made it back to where our house stood. A pogrom that took the lives of 19,000 had just ended, leaving only for the meantime 7,000. Cramped in a smaller ghetto and no freedom to leave it, yet not recalling how I got to our once home, I can't explain.

I entered the grounds and found destruction. The furniture was gone and unidentifiable objects strewn all over. It saddened me only for an instant. After all, what was most important was gone forever. My reason for coming was to retrieve a souvenir, mainly photographs. I knew I should find some. My mother and my sister, Nechamka, were picture-taking enthusiasts. Luckily for me, they were of no value to the looters.

All the pictures were hidden in an inch of face powder. From 1939 to 1941 we were under Russian occupation. Under their system no private enterprise was permitted. Before the liquidation of my father's drugstore, we managed to salvage a few items as huge containers of powder, aromatic soap bars, and such. By the way, those came to very good use when later incarcerated in the ghetto. Food supply was becoming scarce. A Pole would sneak up to the barbed wire fence and exchange a few potatoes for a bar of soap.

The powder boxes torn apart, most likely in search of some hidden treasures, covered the whole floor of our so called 'salon', my mother's pride and joy. On my knees, with my fingers, I combed through the powder and walked away with many pictures of my family. They remained in my two bulging coat pockets until the pockets split open.

When suddenly the next pogrom took place. I instinctively ran to hide, with only the dress I had on. At that time, 6,000 were captured and shut in the ready-mass grave. The remaining 1,000 were 'taken care of' one year later.

Again, as fate chose, I remained among the 1,000 and left alive. Those were only people with trades, put in a smaller yet ghetto. What right did I have to be there? I was, most of the time, out of sight hiding. One year later those too were eradicated. The file 'Judenrein' was closed. At least Poland was then cleansed of Jews.

While still living in that ghetto, the urge to once more visit the sight of our home left me no peace of mind. Risky as it was, I went. My eyes met an entirely different scenario. I saw irony, for the scene was not created by nature, but by human hands.

I felt so sad. The house like other neighbor's houses was gone. Directly on the site where ours stood, somebody had fun. A little mount of the remaining chimney bricks was neatly put together. On top, placed, was one of my father's shoes, one of his socks, one bashed cooking pot, and what pained me more was one of my sister Rivka's slippers neatly hung on the wire-fence that separated the city park and our property. Only our three little cherry trees stood blooming, as if proclaiming, in spite of it all-life goes on...

I came back to the ghetto, 'life' was going on, until began the expected end. Once again, I was spared. A life of hiding, in a stable, then in the forest until the Russian army recaptured our city. Freedom was bittersweet.

In 1945 things came to an end. Among the few survivors, a cousin of mine showed up. He informed me that during the sudden ambush by the Germans, during the first pogrom, my sister Nechamka happened to be in their house across from ours. In panic, she, his father, mother, sister, and brother hid in a most unsafe place where the gaseous fumes asphyxiated them. When the bodies were discovered they were assumed to be buried in a hole near our house. We decided to excavate the bodies and give them a proper burial. We did not find them.

This was the third and last time I revisited that forsaken place. Now when thinking of our house, I try nostalgically to remember all the good years we have spent there. I am left with lots of memories. - Mania Lichtenstein, November 2, 2003

16

LOOKING FOR A NEW HOME

Eventually, they left their hometown and went from city to city. Nobody wanted, needed, or accepted Jews. Anti-Semitism remained frighteningly fierce and prevalent. They had no Jewish home. There was nothing left.

Bubbie remembered hearing that World War II was proclaimed over on May 8, 1945. It was as if another dream came true — they were alive without war!

Despite the declaration of peace, times were dire for the survivors as they had nothing and things were still in chaos. They learned of an organized group in the city of Łódź that was helping survivors regain some dignity and direction and so they made their way there. Many other survivors were also arriving and looking for assistance on where to go and what to do.

Bit by bit, life was becoming a little more livable. They could go to the market and buy food with some gold coins that Moishe and Joseph recovered when they were in their hometown. The gold coins were used to purchase food for all of them — the whole group. At the time, everything was done for the group. Because of everything they'd been through, they adopted more of a 'we' concept, not a selfish 'I' perspective. They were no longer being hunted down, starved, or trapped in a ghetto. The people in the Łódź organization told them about someone traveling from Berlin to Palestine.

Bubbie did not particularly care where they went, as she no longer had feelings, dreams, or desires. She did not really care where they moved to as long as it was a place they could safely call 'home.' Their decision would not be based on a nice climate or a place where one can make a living. Instead, they went where they were let in. They refused, however, to stay in blood-soaked Europe, a region soaked with their own blood and the blood of their families and friends. This was not an option. They would not "step on blood."

They got connected with the United Nations Relief and Rehabilitation Administration (UNRA) and heard of an illegal 'aliya', meaning 'going up,' as in the Jews immigrating to the land of Israel. They decided to go to Palestine, Israel did not exist yet, because this was their homeland.

The first group of Jewish Holocaust survivors, including my grandmother and her family, wanted to go to Palestine but they were rejected. Next, they tried to go to Cyprus, but that attempt failed as well.

In the end, they were forced to return to Eastern Europe where things were slowly returning to some semblance of normalcy. Bubbie and Joseph and Moishe attended the movies, theatre, and the opera. They were young and had their youth. "Like a rosebud," Bubbie said, "First there is a stem and then it is in full bloom."

The sun was shining again after a horrible nightmare that seemed like it would never end. And, although they stayed on German soil, the Germans didn't know they were Jewish unless they told them.

The refugees spoke in German, read books in German, and were otherwise left alone as people assumed they were in fact German.

Joseph and Moishe Lichtenstein (1946).

After the war, Bubbie and Genia Seifert reconnected in their hometown and then again later at a displaced persons (DP) camp called Eshvegen, which was close to Frankfurt. At this time, my grandmother was pregnant with my mother. This picture was taken about that time (male and dog unknown).

My grandmother handwrote this card in Polish to Genia, which translates: "Dear Genia, I'm giving you this picture so you never forget about our comrade / companionship together from our hardship. Mania."

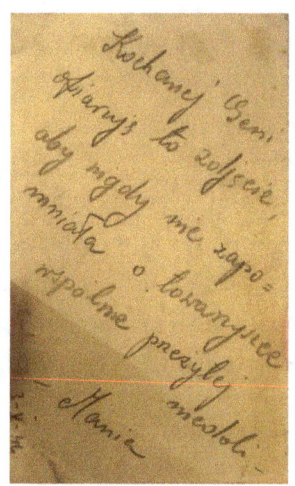

They stayed in Berlin for the next nine months, and then went to a displaced persons refugee camp called Kibbutz Baderach along with a lot of other Jewish survivors. This is where my mother, Guta, was born.

The fourth person from the left is Joseph who is looking at Bubbie.

17

LEAVING 'BLOOD-SOAKED EUROPE'

A couple of friends heard about the birth of my mother and came to see the new baby at Kibbutz Baderach. These friends talked Bubbie and Joseph into moving to Hamburg, telling them that life was quiet there and no one bothered them. Since they had no other place to go and they liked this couple, Bubbie and Joseph agreed and moved there.

Over the next few years, they acclimatized themselves to life in Hamburg. My mother attended school and learned German. Still, they couldn't stay where the "soil was soaked in blood." They wanted to settle somewhere else with their baby and considered a number of different countries and got information about them at displaced persons camps. They also knew of people who were immigrating to Australia, Canada and other destinations.

Adena's mother was born at a DP camp on July 22, 1946.

Dreams

How I long to see my home,
Beyond the ocean, far, far away,
A home that was leveled with all who dwelled in it,
A home once happy and gay.
A home that exists now only in dreams
That let me walk through the door,
And wander from room to room, and reminisce,
Of the years gone by long ago.
The dreams that allow me to see dear faces,
And to their voices to listen,
Pretend that all is the way it was,
And not a thing is missing.
So much would I like to be home once more...
You only my dreams, can open its door.

Mania Lichtenstein, 1995

Adena's mother with her parents, after the war.

I recently discovered the following photo of Bubbie and my mother walking in Berlin after the war. In studying this picture, I am struck by the sense of normalcy it seems to imply. When you know everything that brought them to Berlin, 'normal' seems hardly the right word to use.

Bubbie and Adena's mother walking in Berlin after the war.

18

MOVING TO A NEW COUNTRY

Bubbie's friends, Golde and Misha Zeidman, from one of the displaced persons camps, had immigrated to Canada. They then pretended to be cousins of Bubbie, Joseph, and Moishe, and provided a guarantee to the Canadian Consulate that they would support and be responsible for them. Together Bubbie, Joseph, Moishe, and Guta immigrated by boat to Canada, eventually arriving in Montreal on August 5, 1951.

The Transatlantic voyage took close to two weeks where everyone got sick except for Bubbie as she "had to take care of her child."

On the boat to Montreal. Bubbie and Adena's mother are seated on the far right.

Another family, the Minzbergs who had earlier emigrated from Europe, allowed the four of them to board with them for approximately two weeks. Although they had nothing, they saved as much as they could, knowing that there would be a tomorrow. They saved every penny and before long, many refugees like my grandmother, saved enough to rent an apartment. The four of them were eventually able to get their own flat, a triplex in Outremont, a residential borough of Montreal.

Bubbie did not work outside the home. To be considered a respectable man, Joseph insisted Bubbie stayed home and raise her first child, my mother, Guta. My mother, by the way, was named after her maternal and fraternal mothers, Gitel and her fraternal grandmother pronounced Oodle, although she later changed her name to Jeanie, as she felt Guta sounded too German.

Moishe knew someone who worked for a merchandise wholesaler. This person had emigrated from Poland before the war. He helped Moishe get a job as a shipper. Joseph was not working yet. Later on, Moishe found another job and gave Joseph his job as a shipper. Many immigrants found work this way, by knowing someone who knew someone. Employment was often made based on connections and friendships.

Normal life, at least as normal as it could be, began. Bubbie, however, described it differently, she said that "people really lived in a comatose state." No one wanted to talk about the war or how they had survived. It was a closed book. Everyone just wanted to go on living.

Mania, Joseph and Moise (1945)

Over the years, Moishe and Joseph engaged in several small businesses. They were young, wild, and extremely intelligent. Moishe was self-taught, street-smart, good-hearted and good-natured. They all lived in an apartment building located at 403 St. Joseph Boulevard West in Montreal. They considered their top floor apartment luxurious, as each of them had their own bedrooms. They knew the other families who lived on the same floor and they would often get together to socialize and play card games.

At one point, one of the other boarders, Alex the K., and Moishe started a hat business. They purchased boxes and boxes of hats, which they stored in Moishe's bedroom. My mother told me that as a child, she had so much fun playing dress-up by trying on all the hats, especially the Easter bonnets.

Bubbie and Joseph had a second child about five years after moving to Montreal. My aunt Brenda was named after Joseph and Moishe's baby sister, Branshile in Yiddish.

It was about this time that Moishe opened his first restaurant. It reminded my mom of a country western type of bar. Moishe had an office upstairs where he could look down over the restaurant. He later opened another restaurant in another part of town. Once he was asked why he opened a restaurant during tough times and his response was because "people had to eat." He had a great personality and others were naturally drawn to him. He was considered extremely pragmatic and people often went to him for advice.

Montreal was a Catholic province and it was hard to get a liquor license but Moishe somehow was able to get one. He called his new restaurant Mo-Li (for Morris / Moishe / Monique Lichtenstein). He learned that the money wasn't to be made in the food, but in the alcohol. Moishe once told my mom that rumors spread about how he could obtain a liquor license and some people thought he was connected to the Mafia. He told my mom that it wasn't true, and nothing more was ever said about it. Over the years, he owned several restaurants, all named Mo-Li. The first waitress Moishe ever hired was a French-Canadian woman with an Italian background named Colette Ruth Manelli.

When Brenda was three-and-a-half years old and Jeanie, Guta, thirteen, Joseph died of leukemia, following a six-year-long illness. Initially, the doctor called Moishe and told him about Joseph's diagnosis and the fact that there was no cure. Neither the doctor nor Moishe ever told Joseph or my grandmother. Only two years later, did Moishe tell Bubbie about Joseph's diagnosis.

When Joseph was dying, he asked Moishe to please look after his wife and daughters, which he did faithfully. Moishe really took this responsibility to heart and did more than most fathers do for their own children, emotionally and financially.

Bubbie then had to provide for her two girls, and so a family friend who lived on the floor beneath them recommended that my grandmother become a bookkeeper. So she went back to school to study. During her final exams for school, Brenda got sick and my grandmother wasn't able to take her exams.

Despite this setback, she was hired as a bookkeeper by the company that had previously employed her husband Joseph. She later worked for another company that made winter items such as hats.

In 1967, my mother and father got married. Moishe assumed the role of her father at the wedding.

Adena's mother and Moishe dancing at her wedding.

At the end of the wedding reception, with only the immediate family present, Moishe announced that he planned to marry Colette. My mother learned later that Moishe waited because my father was from an Orthodox family.

Moishe had been worried that my father's family would not allow him to marry off my mother if Moishe married someone who converted to Judaism. So once my mother was married, Moishe announced his intention to marry Colette, which he did two months later on August 20, 1967, his birthday.

Although Moishe and Colette wanted children of their own, they never had any. Most family members believed it was because they could not conceive. I grew up under the impression that it was because Moishe promised Joseph that he would look after his family and thus having children of his own would have been a distraction from this commitment.

In 1970, my father and mother moved to Baltimore, Maryland, so my father could complete a one-year internship in dentistry. I was born there in April of 1971, and Moishe flew to Maryland for one day to see me. Bubbie and Brenda also came and stayed the night.

As a side note, I remember hearing that Moishe met a man who had known his family from before the war. Moishe asked him if he knew what had happened to his parents and younger sister. The man told him that he saw a Nazi with a gun leading them down a street and that he saw them being shot.

I have wonderful memories of visiting my uncle Moishe in Montreal. In his home in Laval, he had a bar downstairs in the basement. I remember he would have my sisters and me sit up on the barstools and he would act like our bartender asking us what 'drink' we would like.

He would offer us 'champagne' which we thought was so extravagant and he would pour a light-colored substance into tall champagne glasses. Of course, we loved it! What kid wouldn't when it was ginger ale and we didn't know any better?

Sometime in the early 1980s, my parents got an early morning phone call from Moishe saying he'd been selected to appear on the television game show *The Price is Right*. It turned out that he and Colette were on their way to Hawaii and had a stopover in Los Angeles. Colette loved the game show and had sent away for tickets. While waiting to get in, according to Moishe, the producers walked the line of attendees to select who they wanted to be a contestant on the show. They asked my uncle what his name was. He said, "Listen, you can call me Moishe, you can call me Morris, you can call me Monique, just call me!"

So, they called him and he was selected to play a golf game. Although he had never picked up a golf club in his life, he swung the club, hit the ball in the hole, and won a Porsche. He ended up going to the Showcase Showdown at the end of the show. He didn't win the Showdown, but he was able to drive away in a new Porsche! As I said earlier, he was a fun person who made people want to be around him.

Sometime during high school, I realized Moishe was not my uncle but actually my great uncle. It struck me as odd because of his deep involvement in my life. I wouldn't have thought that a great uncle would have made such an effort. At my wedding, he walked down the aisle with my grandmother like my grandfather would have.

Bubbie and Moishe at Adena's wedding, 2002.

19

MY ODD WEDDING DAY

Adena and Bubbie (2002)

My grandmother wrote this beautiful piece prior to my wedding:

January 13, 2002, I was present at my granddaughter Adena's bridal shower. I never attended one before. It was lovely and fun. What struck me most observing the attendees was the free and easy mood and manners they displayed. Bursts of continuous, spontaneous laughter filled the room. It was wonderful. It got me thinking how different we, of my generation, were.

I silently prayed that they should never experience hard times, and know to appreciate what they have now. As they were playing games, all pertaining to marriage, my thoughts drifted back to my own odd 'big event.' I can call it odd, but hardly big.

When all were gone, only the family was left. We sat around the kitchen table, enjoying a bite of dessert. My mind was still so full of reminiscence and liked to share it with them. But the time did not seem right; there was too much elation and distractions. As always when unable to talk, I turn to writing. Thanks to my wondrous machine, I can still do it. Here comes my story I so desperately wish to tell.

The date of our wedding was October 15, 1944. The war was not yet over, but the Russian army, finally being on the offensive, reclaimed our city from the Germans and our town was liberated. Emerging from holes we were hiding in, the few survivors surfaced. Free to exist — an unbelievable miracle.

There were very few survivors, young only. We possessed absolutely nothing, not even a picture of families or a document. There was no problem finding a place to live. There were thousands of empty houses whose owners we knew could never return. Everything in the houses was stolen a long time ago. There was a roof and four walls and that was sufficient. Anything was better than what we had for the last several years. The main thing was we were not hunted anymore and we were free and alive.

My husband to be, much more skilful than I, managed to produce some bare necessities for me and as well as for others. No proposal was necessary and "living in sin" was not popular, the wedding date was set. The guest list of six: Bride and Groom, Uncle Moishe, my friend Sue, and an older couple we never knew before. Even if we wanted, we would not come up with more guests. Not all who survived returned at once.

Now being a bride to be, a nice 'new' dress was a must. My wardrobe consisted only of what I had on. Life was still stagnant. Nothing could be bought or obtained, until our market place became a vital trade center.

After a long war, and in need of things or money, this was the place to go. Old clothes and other things were being sold. Folks could buy produce that the farmers supplied in large quantities. There were fruit, eggs, and dairy products. Items we almost forgot existed.

Off I went to the market to purchase my second-hand wedding dress. I was in luck. The dress I found was navy blue with little white felt flowers appliqued around the neck. The more or less fit had to do. I had already two pairs of brown shoes, and was able to give or lend one pair to my friend Sue, who had none so she, too, looked respectable enough for the wedding. Things were going well until we were asked by that married couple on our guest list, "who is giving you away?" there were no existing parents, uncles, or aunts. All were killed. No choice remained, but to let this couple fill in. It was their second marriage, which was against the Jewish law to do it.

Life was upside down then and rules had to be bent. The woman knew how, and baked us a sponge cake. A bottle of vodka was provided, and the menu was complete. One issue remained, to find someone eligible to give us 'chuppa-kedoshim' blessing. Our Rabbi was killed like all the rest.

A man unknown to us with a long, red beard, assured us to be the right person to perform as a Rabbi and to wed us. Hallelujah! We were wed. The "event of the time" took place and it was time to sit back, have a piece of sponge cake, and a L'Chaim schnapps. But it didn't go the way we planned. A reserve of Russian soldiers was stationed in our town. We had no idea how they found out about our party.

Dead drunk already, they burst through the door and finished off the vodka in their drunken stupor. They demanded to tell them who is the bride. How could they have recognized who might the bride in her navy-blue dress be?

My husband swiftly whisked me off to another room. Imprisoned in a locked room on my big day. Scared to death, for they never stopped banging on the door, urging me to come out. Drunk to exhaustion, they finally left and I was liberated once again. The tragi-comedy of a wedding ended.

I was married for sixteen years only before it tragically ended. But on a brighter note — like the Phoenix rising from the ashes — two dear daughters came forth, hence, five wonderfully special granddaughters who are my pride and joy. May they know only happiness. I am anticipating their weddings, which naturally will look much different than mine. - Mania Lichtenstein, January 16, 2002

Bubbie often seemed to me to be torn between two realities— her own past and her family's present, especially mine, perhaps because I was her oldest grandchild. I know how happy she was to be at my wedding, but it is obvious from her writings how she was drawn back to the memories of her unexpected experience at her own wedding. She had the courage to be present for me and partake in the joyous celebration, yet she still struggled with flashbacks from her past. This is truly a testament to her strength and her grace.

I was the first of her granddaughters to get pregnant, and I am sure you can imagine the surprise and delight when she heard I was having twins. That, coupled with me being pregnant with a boy, the first in three generations, was all very exciting for her. She wrote this for us:

May this tree always be well and strong

To Adena and Brad, Sarah and Zachari.
Two 'family trees' with two different names,
Grew far removed from each other.
Never dreaming of joining its branches,
That could make them heartily gladder.
Treated with love and great care.
The way trees seem to flourish and strive,
On their branches — no wonder —
two blossoms appeared,
Announcing great happiness is about to arrive.
And now these blossoms are branches,
They are joining this fabulous tree,
To add to it more pride and happiness,
And indescribable glee.

Mania Lichtenstein, January 19, 2004

20

RIGHTEOUS AMONG THE NATIONS

When local organizations ask me to speak about my grandmother's story I am often asked about Popa. Unfortunately, I do not know too much about her. What I do know is that she and my grandmother fled from the final ghetto to Janina Zawadzka's home. From there, they traveled to the forest where they were eventually liberated. When my grandmother moved to Montreal, Popa moved to New York. She had two girls and has since passed away.

Since embarking on the endeavor of writing this book, I have also nominated Janina Zawadzka to be considered for the Righteous Among the Nations, a list used by the State of Israel to honor non-Jews who put their own lives in peril during the Holocaust to save Jews from extermination by the Nazis.

Over the course of several months, I completed and submitted a nomination for Janina Zawadzka as she was a defender of the defenseless and a protector of the hopeless. She risked her life to help save Bubbie and Popa. I received a response from Yad Vashem in July 2019 indicating that one of the principal duties of Yad

Vashem is to convey the gratitude of the Jewish people to those non-Jews who risked their lives to save Jews during the Holocaust.

The Commission, which designates the title of the Righteous, is headed by a Supreme Court Judge and operates according to a clear set of criteria and regulations. Each case is meticulously researched and needs to be substantiated by evidence establishing the rescue efforts and the circumstances. One of the basic requirements is to have testimonies of the survivors or persons that were helped that describe the circumstances of the rescue and the nature of the help that was extended. The commission then goes on to examine whether the aid falls within the criteria for awarding the title. They have asked me to be patient as the process could take many months.

Additionally, my connection with Genia Seifert, the woman who lived in the ghetto with my grandmother, led to another nomination of the Polish woman that saved her: Maria Domovsky. She also has now been nominated to be included in the list of Righteous Among the Nations.

My grandmother said that this war was not an easy one to forget. The survivors go through the motions of life and pretend to be normal people, but regretfully, they are not.

She wrote, "How can one forget all this gore?" A friend of hers, also a survivor, told my grandmother, "Do you realize that we are unable to laugh?" My grandmother confirmed this was true. She continued that, aside from the pain of losing everything, there is also an enormous feeling of shame. She said, "It is one thing to be killed in a war but another to be slaughtered like sheep. One's ego suffers." And such was the mentality of the Eastern European Jews, always afraid, always the victim.

So, how did my Bubbie survive? She felt that she survived because of fate. She once wrote, "I am riddled with that same, always nagging question, 'why was I spared?' Every time I found myself in a situation of life or death, an invisible hand would pull me out of harm's way. My thinking or actions had absolutely nothing to do with it; fate guided me."

She also wrote, "It can plainly be seen that fate made me avoid all those disastrous situations. I and the other survivors were meant to survive so we could remind the world of the atrocities committed and also tell the world that there once existed in Europe a rich Jewish life and culture, which due to one man's madness, was extinguished."

But in knowing her story and reading her writings, it wasn't all just pure luck or miracles. My Bubbie was very resourceful and found ways out of horrible situations. While she admitted that she was the most naïve and the youngest of her family, she was insightful enough to think of people to go to, resources to use, and strategies to employ.

It was a desperate time that called for desperate measures, and while luck and fate may have been on her side, she also made careful and good decisions that proved to benefit her tremendously. She said, "In my misfortune, I was very lucky."

Her experiences affected her children and, as a result, they never felt like anybody else. They noticed the lack of cousins, aunts and uncles, and my grandmother did not have an easy explanation as to why those relatives didn't exist.

Bubbie told me that what she lived through and experienced, it made her appreciate what she has, even insignificant things. Her advice for future generations is to treasure family, to live in harmony, and to respect one another. Having one less dress is not important. Instead, what is important is having a roof over your head and being able to eat. Appreciate what you have.

For most of my professional life, I have been involved in criminal prosecution working for the government. I work for one of the largest prosecution offices in the country.

Although I have worked in many bureaus of my office, most of my work has involved victim-crimes. I found this quote by Elie Wiesel to be so applicable not only to my work as a prosecutor, but as something I have focused on in the seventh grade Sunday School Holocaust Studies class taught at Temple Solel in Paradise Valley, Arizona. We must always be an *upstander*, not a *bystander*. By that I mean, we must stand up against injustice and use our voices. We must defend the defenseless and be a protector of the hopeless.

> We must always take sides.
> Neutrality helps the oppressor,
> never the victim.
> Silence encourages the tormentor,
> never the tormented.
> - Elie Wiesel

Equally important to me, is the duty to carry on the traditions of my ancestors. All three of my children have been named after those who have since parted. At their baby naming ceremonies, and again at their Bar and Bat Mitzvahs, we discussed who those people were and the influence they have had on their father and me. At each of their Bar and Bat Mitzvahs, we talked about the prayer for our children to live long lives filled with peace, health, lots of laughter, happiness and purpose, while surrounded by family, friends, and community.

Likewise, we also discussed the promise the children hold — one which is filled with values and traditions of all those who came before us, who we cherish and respect such as lighting the candlesticks every Friday night to welcome the Sabbath.

As a mother, it is my hope that the values and traditions of my children's grandparents, and their parents, and the parents before them, will guide my children in their lives; values of family, of community, of living a life with a purpose and dignity, performing good deeds or *mitzvot*. Just like my grandmother's grandmother's act of giving her the pickle in hopes that it might sustain my grandmother for a few more days, we pass along our love through supporting each other, sharing family stories, and being there for each other.

Learning the details of my grandmother's story of survival from the Holocaust was not easy. It evoked many emotions — those of loss, fear, horror, tragedy, and many others. Bubbie told me that telling her story was definitely not her pleasure, but she felt it was her duty, and I feel it is mine, as well.

21

MORE OF MANIA'S WRITINGS

Tender Reflections amidst Dark Days

This sheet of paper before me, pen in hand, low-vision-aid machine is on, and I am ready to pour my heart out. Yet I halt and reflect, should I? So many times in the past I was asked, rather critically, "Why do you write, why live in the past?" The following example might answer such a question.

Like a raised dam would release sheets of gushing water, so does my mind, after years of suppressed memories, sets loose many thoughts impossible to forget. Yes! I'll continue writing as long as I can. What prompted me to write this time are two incidents, which to this day make my eyes well up with tears, when thinking of them.

One relates to my grandmother, the other to a noble elderly man. After more than one year behind barbed wires, we in our ghetto reached the limit of endurance and our food supply. No new sources were existing. Everybody felt hungry.

For the last three days before the extermination would begin, a selection of hundreds of young women took place. I and the others were to harvest in the fields. The job so alien to us, we learned quickly, due to the German overseer's swift whip.

On the third day, prior to leaving for work, my grandmother, whom I loved dearly, handed me a tiny, sour pickle somebody gave to her. She knew there was nothing else I can take along. She insisted I take it. It moved me greatly, for I realized that she, too, was hungry. One might say, "What a banality — a pickle!" a miniscule, tiny pickle could taste so good when nothing else is available. To me that selfless act was a token of her love for me. I remember it with tenderness.

I was never to see her again, nor any member of my family. Our apocalypse had begun. After the third day of work ended, we were brought back to one of the two existing ghettos. It was not the one where my family lived. Forbidden to cross over to our ghetto, I had to find shelter for the night with my sister's in-laws.

The next day at 6 a.m., the first pogrom began, which lasted fifteen days. Caught by the sudden ambush, all in that building ran to hide in its attic. We felt like being fried under the extremely hot tin roof. We had no food or water. For the first few days, nibbling on raw potatoes sustained us. In later days, food was not even desired.

Today I find it hard to believe, but it is true. The lack of water became our major problem. To survive without it was inconceivable. Not knowing how much longer that human hunt might last, we were already dried up to half our weight.

We began to wonder if the end of our life would feel easier. It was the eighth day of the pogrom, the horrid noises from outside subsided a little. The desired number of 19,000 Jews was almost reached. It became much quieter than in the earlier days. Remembering a dish with rainwater on one of the balconies was too tempting to ignore. One took the risk to go out and get it. The safe return with that dish of stale rainwater was never to be forgotten.

We all had a turn to get a few sips of that lifesaving delicacy. When my sister's father-in-law was to have his few sips, he refused and in a hardly audible voice whispered, "Let the children have it," namely I and a niece of his. He insisted and we drank his share. I wish we hadn't, for those few sips of water could have saved that kind man's life.

We had no more water to drink until the fifteenth day of our ordeal. 19,000 Jews were caught, shot, and buried in mass graves that were dug earlier. Two months later, six thousand more followed. All of our town's Jews were dead, but for one thousand. For one year we provided for the Germans any tasks they required. After one year, the inevitable came.

After the first fifteen-days-pogrom, our group from the attic emerged. Skeleton-like but alive. If only for the meantime, we held on bewildered. It was not so for my sister's father-in-law. He emerged, but a day later he quietly succumbed. Dehydration took its toll. He sacrificed his few sips of water, so we, the children, would have a better chance to survive. I will always cherish the memory of that fine, gentle man.

For me, and those like me, it is quite hard to erase the memories of those dark, hard to imagine experiences. - Mania Lichtenstein, October 26, 2002

Memories that won't go away

In the still of the night sleep does not come, There's pain in my head, and pounding of heart. I see, I hear, I feel their pain, Back then, when the world seemed clearly insane. In 1942, from the clear autumn sky, God looked down on us, not blinking an eye. They were caught like stray dogs, and loaded on trucks, Mothers, fathers, little babies, and scared tiny tots, Wishing to know what their big crime was, They well could tell where the road led to: To the place called PIATYDNIE, they so well knew. The place where mass graves stood empty and big, Just a few weeks earlier, Jews were ordered to dig. Mothers looking at children with apologizing eyes, "Sorry my little ones" seemed spelling their sighs.

The one-way journey soon came to an end, Facing the beast-man-made craters, Knowing well what they meant. "Hurry up," they roared, "Jump in, you pigs," Nineteen thousand this time must fill these digs.

Lucky were those quickly shot and dead, The others drowned slowly in a blood-filled bed. Mission accomplished —POGROM #1- GREAT SUCCESS!

And two months later #2 will progress. Six thousand only, a task easy next time, With perfect planning, will take place right on time. Same trucks, same route, destination well known, To the thought of death, accustomed they've grown. Their fate was sealed, no change to regress (redress?) POGROM #2-YET ANOTHER SUCCESS

One thousand was left, but for only one year. To produce for the Germans their much-needed gear. After one year and one month to be precise, The thousand's fate was no surprise. One town reached 'perfection' with JUDENREIN *The Nazis were gloating with genuine pride. And this took place in my home town* WLODZIMIERZ.

From Polish towns, like mine, for one, The Jews were wiped out, and forever gone. It was painful for me to write this piece. But I felt I had placed at their graves a wreath...

Easy sleep will never come, For I can't forget and overcome...

Mania Lichtenstein

Life

Years go by so slowly,
Yet move on so fast,
A day seems to last forever,
But does not last.
Each moment has a beginning,
That shapes our day or mind,
Albeit, a beginning, as we know it,
Must always have an end.
Laughter, bliss, and happiness,
how lovely these words sound,
But without tears and suffering,
Appreciation is never found.
The good, the bad, the happy and sad,
Are all tied up as one,
In the journey of life that begins one day
Till its time runs out-someday
Once again new life starts to play its parts
In this perpetual cycle of LIFE.

Mania Lichtenstein, 1997

1942 — A Flashback

Memories. Why must they keep coming back? I sometimes forget what I did yesterday, yet things that happened years ago keep flashing before my eyes. If they could only be rinsed away with the tears that they cause! The fact remains, they constantly come back filling my heart with too much sadness.

I keep these thoughts to myself. Why upset or maybe bore others with something they can't even relate to. Here you come in, my dear paper and pen... I am grateful to the especially designed paper and the 'Aladdin' that make it possible for me to write. You listen when I open my heart; it helps me a bit.

Today I had a flashback of 1942. The years that followed were not in any way easier. Robbed of feelings, as if in a comatose state, all I wanted was for this nightmare to be over. Come what may!

Today my thoughts go back to September 1, 1942. The first chapter of the infamous extermination of our ghetto. At 6 a.m., when the first shots rang out, I found myself separated from my family. Caught off guard, in panic, I followed some people to an attic where we spent fifteen days, the duration of the first pogrom! Since this happened in an instant, no food or drink was brought in. In a squatting position, trying as far as possible to distance oneself from the extremely hot tin roof we motionlessly waited, hardly uttering a word.

The search was intense. The stomping of the Nazi boots on the roof as they were looking for their 'precious prey' was exploding our nerves. Not for an instant did anybody think or desire food. Water... this was another thing! One can only imagine what lack of water can do to a person! Some started losing their mind and began acting erratically.

On the eighth day of dryness, getting a drink of water became a must. One of us crawled out of hiding to get a dish of rain water from one of the balconies because there was no running water in this building.

That sip of stale water would not be forgotten for many years to come. Water, the most precious jewel in life.

In the meantime, looking through the spaces between the boards of the attic, I watched the flames from the ghetto, where my family was. It was no use fooling myself. It was not hard to guess their fate. They had already joined the 19,000 destined to perish in that pogrom. The prepared mass graves had already swallowed the flesh and blood of innocent men, women, and little ones. The clothes they had to remove before being murdered had surely more value to the Nazis than Jewish lives.

It took two more pogroms after that one to eliminate the 26,000 Jews living in my hometown. 'Judenrein', clean of Jews, was their 'noble cause.' People sometimes say, don't dwell on the past. Easy said, I can't, though I try. The flashbacks will happen forever!

Mania Lichtenstein, August 23, 1998

To See

To see makes you feel that the world is yours,
Yours to behold its splendor and beauty,
The sky of blue with the sun shining through,
Or dark night's sky strewn with silver,
To see faces you know, your own, or new ones you meet,
Not much a recognized pleasure,
Unless when sight is sadly gone,
One begins to bemoan the lost treasure,
The world once yours slowly slips away,
Becoming a distant memory.

Mania Lichtenstein, December 31, 2002
(written in a moment of frustration)

Time Phenomenon

The sun slid behind the horizon,
Proclaiming a day has gone by.
Not to worry. Another day is in the making,
To appear next day, in the hour of waking.
For time never stops,
no power can do,
Magic can't stop it for a second or two.
Every second gone by is gone forever,
It never stops or repeats itself-ever!
The clock. A device fashioned after time,
Keeps tick-tocking constantly on,
The tick-tock just heard,
we won't hear again,
It's been swallowed by the never resting time,
Each morning we face a brand-new beginning,
We move in step with eternal time
Whatever we do, might cease one day,
But time... will be marching on...

Mania Lichtenstein, May 2001

The Nostalgic Past

I am an emotional person, anyone who knows me, will agree. When I was young, emotions, reflections of the past had to be suppressed. Taking care of children, a steady, demanding job, and the unexpected, that life so often presented, was enough to fill my mind.

There were often flashes of the years gone by, still very vivid in my memory, but those were quickly brushed aside. For the moment, pretending that the past never existed, helped to endure. Now being at a different stage in my life, and having ample idle time on my hands, there is nothing that could deter my emotions and thoughts from running amok.

I think of my family, people I have known in the past, who all perished, leaving me with so many unanswered questions. They are gone and now it is too late...

Young people are not aware of the mistake they are making by not hungering for their elders' past. After all, it's theirs as well. Their lives could be so richly endowed by that knowledge.

'A lifetime,' sounds like an eternity, yet it goes by rather quickly. When one is old and looks back, all seems to have happened just 'yesterday.' The past is an inseparable part of us, and always bring back a heavy dose of nostalgia.

Mania Lichtenstein, December 26, 1999

1997: The Years of Fear

(*Letter in Yiddish translated into English*)

Long gone are the years,
long gone is time,
When I was a child,
equal with all the other children,

With one mother and one father,
sisters' laughter was heard,
Not believing that sometime
this will all be disrupted.
One dark cloud came and covered the sky,
Ordered that the Jewish nation

must be removed from the world.
Shooting, burning, they made fools of us
Not one memory should remain,
the dark clouds thought.
Laughing when a mother shed bloody tears
Watching how her children's blood was spilled
She too, was soon taken away from this angry world
Thinking that no one would survive this scare
Who will tell the world all of this?
So hard to understand,
she (the world) will surely not believe it!
In this black cloud a dot of light appeared
Therefore, I stayed alive for others
Not to allow it to be forgotten,
to tell, to remind
How everything disappeared,
and how everything got forlorn.
After so many years, not a day goes by
That I can forget the years of fear
To forget...
Not possible although I want to a little bit
We won't allow it again
— Jewish blood to be sprinkled from knives!

Mania Lichtenstein

The Mountain We Climb

The steep life's mountain we climb
From the very first day of our life
A mountain so tempting and rugged
We are prompted by some magnetic drive.
Slowly ascending, every step a struggle,
We climb on, as we must, to the top,

Scratched, bruised, aching or worse
Life's rules urge us not to stop.
So, on we go through the good times and bad,
At times we are sliding or falling,
We still are young, plenty energy left
Nature's force orders us to keep moving.
Then one day, a bit tired, we reach the zenith,
Take a moment to rest and reflect,
Looking back at the trail we left behind
Counting the years spent building our nest.
We wonder when all that time went by,
Smiling at our achievements,
Regretting the things not done right,
To change or repair we cannot.
Too late, what's done is done,
Our downhill journey awaits,
With less drive and aching limbs
We slowly begin to descend.
The rules of life's mountain hold fast nor won't bend,
Exhausted from the nonstop climb,
What's left of our days we try to enjoy,
Till peace eternal would come.

Mania Lichtenstein, January 16, 2003

The future consists of: dreams and hope,
The past of: memories and reminiscences!

The Artist Supreme

*All through the ages, artists created
Objects of beauty, so real,
Reflecting nature in all its glory,
And faces that "live and feel."
As we walk through the halls where their art is shown,
In awe we stand and adore,
Dresses of velvet, silk, and lace,
Elegantly touching the floor.
Men were created in God's image, they say
He no doubt has been their mentor,
He made them see the wonders around them,
Spread with abundant luster
He made them aware of the pale-blue sky,
That changes its dress for the night,
To a midnight-blue adorned with stars,
To be seen from near and far.
The deep green meadows dotted with flowers,
Of pink, red, yellow, or white,
He told them to look at the rainbow of colors,
To behold that wonderful sight.
The shy little violets that appear at woods' edges,
Again and again each spring,
And not to ignore the gold of the sun,
And the silvery shine of the moon.
The black of the night and white of snow,
Exist in spite of their gloom,
The anatomy's precision of all living things,
Perhaps... the greatest wonder we know!!!
All of these blended in a perfect theme,
Made for us all by an 'Artist Supreme.'
He granted just a few the skill to emulate
The wonders of his creation,*

But only on canvas with paint and brush,
Attempt-a duplication.
Let the Bible and Darwin argue who's right,
It matters not much to me,
I look around me and without doubt,
A masterpiece I see.

Mania Lichtenstein, 1998

(*When the prognosis of my eyes sounded bad, I came out on the patio and saw beauty, I hardly noticed before.*)

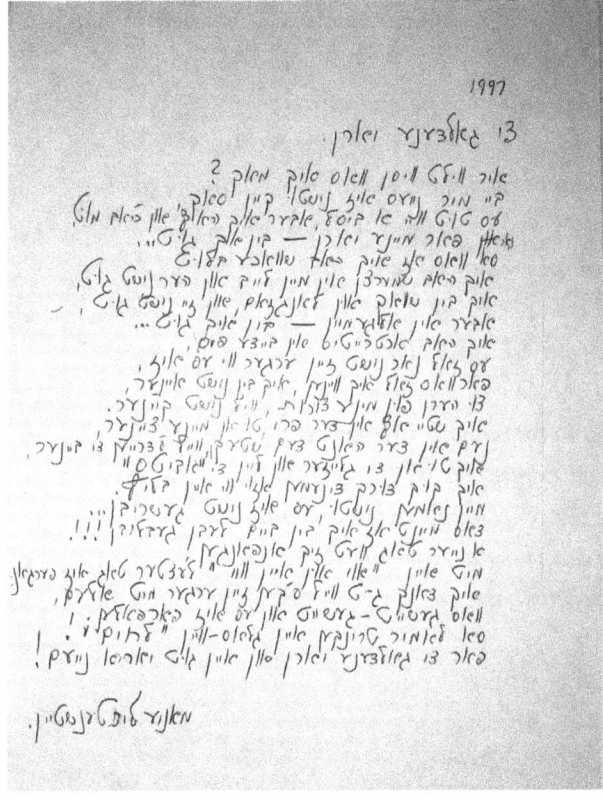

Letter in Yiddish

1997: The Golden Years
(*Letter in Yiddish translated into English*)

Would you like to know how I'm doing?
By me, there isn't much news
It hurts a little, but I have hope and desire
But for my age, I'm good.
So what if I have weak blood
I have pain in my body, and I don't hear well
I am weak and slow, and don't see well
But all in all, I am good.
I have arthritis in both legs
It should only not get worse than it is!
Why should I cry, I'm not the only one.
To hear of my troubles, no one wants.
I wake up in the morning, put on my teeth,
take my cane in my hand because my bones are aching,
I put on my glasses and read the obituaries,
I look through the names like a flash
My name is not there, it is not written,
This means that I am still alive.
A new day will begin
With an Oy vey, the last day passed
I thank G-d because everything could be worse
What happened, happened, it is bygone
So let's drink one glass of wine - l'chaim
For the golden years, and a new good year!

Mania Lichtenstein

POSTSCRIPT

It is no surprise that my grandmother found it difficult and deeply painful to record her observations and experiences of the war, about the horror, and about the unimaginable losses.

Towards the end, she wrote:

> *After finishing the last story I wrote, I vowed it would be the last time I wrote. My failing eyesight could not cooperate any longer.*
>
> *Yet, here I write again... idle time, of which I have plenty, induces the mind to dig up memories of a lifetime. They fill the mind beyond capacity, and to ease it, I must write, as difficult as it may be!*
>
> *Writing this was not easy and has cost me several sleepless nights. It is done now, and hopefully, never again will a Jew have to experience such hell.*

– Mania Lichtenstein

At the time I was writing *Living among the Dead*, I simultaneously submitted Janina Zawadzka's name for Yad Vashem's Righteous Among the Nations. Righteous Among the Nations is a list of non-Jewish individuals who have been honored by Yad Vashem, Israel's Holocaust memorial, for risking their lives to aid Jews during the Holocaust. In December of 2020 I received a letter from Yad Vashem stating that Janina Zawadzka was awarded the honor and her name is now displayed in the garden at Yad Vashem along with the other Righteous honorees.

During the summer of 2021, a unique opportunity was bestowed upon me and I found myself traveling to my grandmother's hometown, now located in western Ukraine. Prior to the trip it was really impossible for me to imagine the area my grandmother talked about. However, the black and white images that occupied my head were soon filled in with color and depth; the sunflowers I pictured in my mind's eye physically engulfed me in their massive fields. The trip included time spent on her street, finding the lot where we believed her house once stood.

I tried to picture what it must have been like for my grandmother to grow up in that area surrounded by her family, playing in the street with her friends and smelling the beautiful flowers. I looked up at the sky and wondered if I could be looking at the same space she saw as a child. Did she ever look up, when it was dark and starry, and make a wish? I asked myself, if so, how could a wish-filled sky become so dark and ugly?

During my time in her hometown, I met some of the most wonderful people I could imagine. Neighbors living on her street asked me to stop by and introduce myself. We ate cherries off the trees and apricots off the vines. I visited the mass graves my grandmother spoke of, discovering there were three graves, not the two she discussed. The timing of my trip couldn't have been at a better time as Russia invaded Ukraine only seven months later.

The plot of land where we believe my grandmother's family's home once stood.

Adena walking to the site of the mass graves.

The third grave we walked to, believed to be filled first in time with Jewish men, women, and children. It is my belief my grandmother's family was buried in this grave as they were murdered during the first pogrom.

REVIEW REQUEST

It is my sincere hope that reading my grandmother's story has increased your knowledge and understanding of the Holocaust. It would be greatly appreciated if you would submit a short review on Amazon or on Goodreads. That would offer greater exposure for my grandmother's story.

Many thanks in advance!

Adena Bernstein Astrowsky

For enquiries about lectures
please get in touch with the author:

adena.astrowsky@gmail.com

For enquiries about bulk orders for book club discussions or classrooms, or for author's manuscripts, please get in touch with Liesbeth Heenk of Amsterdam Publishers:

info@amsterdampublishers.com

Together with Hilary Levine I created an Educator's Guide to accompany this book.

It is available on Amazon (Kindle and paperback):

Living among the Dead: My Grandmother's Holocaust Story of Love and Strength - EDUCATOR'S GUIDE.

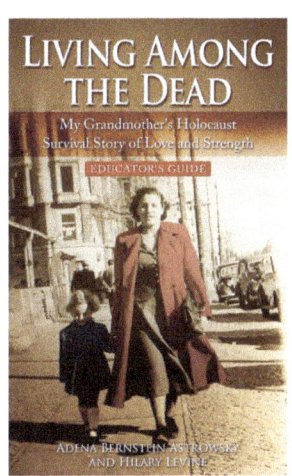

NOTES

5. Life in Poland

1. https://www.chabad.org/library/article_cdo/aid/3025072/jewish/What-Is-a-Shtetl-The-Jewish-Town.htm
2. Yitzkor is a memorial service held by Jews on certain holy days for deceased relatives.
3. https://www.facinghistory.org/holocaust-and-human-behavior/chapter-6/joining-hitler-youth
4. https://www.history.com/news/how-the-hitler-youth-turned-a-generation-of-kids-into-nazis

6. Russian Control

1. https://www.jewishgen.org/Yizkor/Volodymyr_Volynskyy/vol022.html
2. https://encyclopedia.ushmm.org/content/en/article/nazi-propaganda
3. idem
4. https://www.jewishgen.org/Yizkor/Volodymyr_Volynskyy/vol022.html

7. Unforgettable Images

1. https://www.jewishgen.org/Yizkor/Volodymyr_Volynskyy/vol022.html
2. Idem
3. https://encyclopedia.ushmm.org/content/en/article/forced-labor
4. https://www.yadvashem.org/untoldstories/database/index.asp?cid=1043
5. https://www.jewishgen.org/Yizkor/Volodymyr_Volynskyy/vol022.html
6. Idem
7. http://www.yivoencyclopedia.org/article.aspx/Ghettos/Ghetto_Police

8. German Occupation

1. https://www.jewishgen.org/Yizkor/Volodymyr_Volynskyy/vol022.html
2. The Jewish calendar is based on lunar cycles. Therefore, holidays occur on different dates each year of the solar calendar.

9. The Beginning of the End

1. https://www.jewishgen.org/Yizkor/Volodymyr_Volynskyy/vol022.html

2. https://www.myjewishlearning.com/article/what-were-pogroms/
3. https://www.jewishgen.org/Yizkor/Volodymyr_Volynskyy/Volodymyr_Volynskyy.html
4. https://encyclopedia.ushmm.org/content/en/article/einsatzgruppen
5. https://encyclopedia.ushmm.org/content/en/article/the-final-solution
6. https://encyclopedia.ushmm.org/content/en/article/einsatzgruppen
7. Michael Berenbaum, *The World Must Know*, Johns Hopkins University Press; Revised edition (January 2006), p. 92.
8. Ibidem, pp. 100-101.
9. Ibidem, p. 93.
10. https://www.jewishvirtuallibrary.org/babi-yar
    http://www.holocaustresearchproject.org/einsatz/babiyar.html
    Michael Berenbaum, Johns Hopkins University Press; Revised edition (January 2006), p. 98.
11. https://encyclopedia.ushmm.org/content/en/article/final-solution-in-depth
12. https://www.yadvashem.org/untoldstories/documents/From_Report_Einsatzgruppen_Extermination.pdf
13. https://www.jewishgen.org/Yizkor/Volodymyr_Volynskyy/volo22.html
14. Idem
15. Idem
16. https://www.chabad.org/library/article_cdo/aid/705353/jewish/The-Shema.htm
17. https://www.jewishgen.org/Yizkor/Volodymyr_Volynskyy/volo22.html
18. http://chelm.freeyellow.com/ludmir.html

10. Life in the Attic

1. https://www.jewishgen.org/Yizkor/Volodymyr_Volynskyy/volo22.html
2. Idem
3. Idem
4. Idem

11. A New Ghetto

1. Idem
2. http://chelm.freeyellow.com/austila.html,
   http://chelm.freeyellow.com/piatydni.html

12. One Thousand Remaining

1. https://www.jewishgen.org/Yizkor/Volodymyr_Volynskyy/volo22.html
2. Idem.

14. Liberation

1. Idem
2. https://www.yadvashem.org/untoldstories/database/index.asp?cid=1043

AMSTERDAM PUBLISHERS HOLOCAUST LIBRARY

The series **Holocaust Survivor Memoirs World War II** consists of the following autobiographies of survivors:

Outcry. Holocaust Memoirs, by Manny Steinberg

Hank Brodt Holocaust Memoirs. A Candle and a Promise, by Deborah Donnelly

The Dead Years. Holocaust Memoirs, by Joseph Schupack

Rescued from the Ashes. The Diary of Leokadia Schmidt, Survivor of the Warsaw Ghetto, by Leokadia Schmidt

My Lvov. Holocaust Memoir of a twelve-year-old Girl, by Janina Hescheles

Remembering Ravensbrück. From Holocaust to Healing, by Natalie Hess

Wolf. A Story of Hate, by Zeev Scheinwald with Ella Scheinwald

Save my Children. An Astonishing Tale of Survival and its Unlikely Hero, by Leon Kleiner with Edwin Stepp

Holocaust Memoirs of a Bergen-Belsen Survivor & Classmate of Anne Frank, by Nanette Blitz Konig

Defiant German - Defiant Jew. A Holocaust Memoir from inside the Third Reich, by Walter Leopold with Les Leopold

In a Land of Forest and Darkness. The Holocaust Story of two Jewish Partisans, by Sara Lustigman Omelinski

Holocaust Memories. Annihilation and Survival in Slovakia, by Paul Davidovits

From Auschwitz with Love. The Inspiring Memoir of Two Sisters' Survival, Devotion and Triumph Told by Manci Grunberger Beran & Ruth Grunberger Mermelstein, by Daniel Seymour

Remetz. Resistance Fighter and Survivor of the Warsaw Ghetto, by Jan Yohay Remetz

My March Through Hell. A Young Girl's Terrifying Journey to Survival, by Halina Kleiner with Edwin Stepp

Roman's Journey, by Roman Halter

Beyond Borders. Escaping the Holocaust and Fighting the Nazis. 1938-1948, by Rudi Haymann

The Engineers. A memoir of survival through World War II in Poland and Hungary, by Henry Reiss

Spark of Hope. An Autobiography, by Luba Wrobel Goldberg

Footnote to History. From Hungary to America. The Memoir of a Holocaust Survivor, by Andrew Laszlo

The Courtyard. A memoir, by Ben Parket and Alexa Morris

Run, Mendel Run, by Milton H. Schwartz

The series **Holocaust Survivor True Stories**
consists of the following biographies:

Among the Reeds. The true story of how a family survived the Holocaust, by Tammy Bottner

A Holocaust Memoir of Love & Resilience. Mama's Survival from Lithuania to America, by Ettie Zilber

Living among the Dead. My Grandmother's Holocaust Survival Story of Love and Strength, by Adena Bernstein Astrowsky

Heart Songs. A Holocaust Memoir, by Barbara Gilford

Shoes of the Shoah. The Tomorrow of Yesterday, by Dorothy Pierce

Hidden in Berlin. A Holocaust Memoir, by Evelyn Joseph Grossman

Separated Together. The Incredible True WWII Story of Soulmates Stranded an Ocean Apart, by Kenneth P. Price, Ph.D.

The Man Across the River. The incredible story of one man's will to survive the Holocaust, by Zvi Wiesenfeld

If Anyone Calls, Tell Them I Died. A Memoir, by Emanuel (Manu) Rosen

The House on Thrömerstrasse. A Story of Rebirth and Renewal in the Wake of the Holocaust, by Ron Vincent

Dancing with my Father. His hidden past. Her quest for truth. How Nazi Vienna shaped a family's identity, by Jo Sorochinsky

The Story Keeper. Weaving the Threads of Time and Memory - A Memoir, by Fred Feldman

Krisia's Silence. The Girl who was not on Schindler's List, by Ronny Hein

Defying Death on the Danube. A Holocaust Survival Story, by Debbie J. Callahan with Henry Stern

A Doorway to Heroism. A decorated German-Jewish Soldier who became an American Hero, by W. Jack Romberg

The Shoemaker's Son. The Life of a Holocaust Resister, by Laura Beth Bakst

The Redhead of Auschwitz. A True Story, by Nechama Birnbaum

Land of Many Bridges. My Father's Story, by Bela Ruth Samuel Tenenholtz

Creating Beauty from the Abyss. The Amazing Story of Sam Herciger, Auschwitz Survivor and Artist, by Lesley Ann Richardson

On Sunny Days We Sang. A Holocaust Story of Survival and Resilience, by Jeannette Grunhaus de Gelman

Painful Joy. A Holocaust Family Memoir, by Max J. Friedman

I Give You My Heart. A True Story of Courage and Survival, by Wendy Holden

In the Time of Madmen, by Mark A. Prelas

Monsters and Miracles. Horror, Heroes and the Holocaust, by Ira Wesley Kitmacher

Flower of Vlora. Growing up Jewish in Communist Albania, by Anna Kohen

Aftermath: Coming of Age on Three Continents. A Memoir, by Annette Libeskind Berkovits

Not a real Enemy. The True Story of a Hungarian Jewish Man's Fight for Freedom, by Robert Wolf

Zaidy's War. Four Armies, Three Continents, Two Brothers. One Man's Impossible Story of Endurance, by Martin Bodek

The Glassmaker's Son. Looking for the World my Father left behind in Nazi Germany, by Peter Kupfer

The Apprentice of Buchenwald. The True Story of the Teenage Boy Who Sabotaged Hitler's War Machine, by Oren Schneider

Good for a Single Journey, by Helen Joyce

Burying the Ghosts. She escaped Nazi Germany only to have her life torn apart by the woman she saved from the camps: her mother, by Sonia Case

American Wolf. From Nazi Refugee to American Spy. A True Story, by Audrey Birnbaum

Bipolar Refugee. A Saga of Survival and Resilience, by Peter Wiesner

In the Wake of Madness. My Family's Escape from the Nazis, by Bettie Lennett Denny

Before the Beginning and After the End, by Hymie Anisman

I Will Give Them an Everlasting Name. Jacksonville's Stories of the Holocaust, by Samuel Cox

Hiding in Holland. A Resistance Memoir, by Shulamit Reinharz

The Ghosts on the Wall. A Grandson's Memoir of the Holocaust, by Kenneth D. Wald

Thirteen in Auschwitz. My grandmother's fight to stay human, by Lauren Meyerowitz Port

The series **Jewish Children in the Holocaust** consists of the
following autobiographies of Jewish children
hidden during WWII in the Netherlands:

Searching for Home. The Impact of WWII on a Hidden Child,
by Joseph Gosler

Sounds from Silence. Reflections of a Child Holocaust Survivor,
Psychiatrist and Teacher, by Robert Krell

Sabine's Odyssey. A Hidden Child and her Dutch Rescuers,
by Agnes Schipper

The Journey of a Hidden Child, by Harry Pila and Robin Black

The series **New Jewish Fiction** consists of the following novels, written by Jewish authors. All novels are set in the time during or after the Holocaust.

The Corset Maker. A Novel, by Annette Libeskind Berkovits

Escaping the Whale. The Holocaust is over. But is it ever over for the next generation? by Ruth Rotkowitz

When the Music Stopped. Willy Rosen's Holocaust, by Casey Hayes

Hands of Gold. One Man's Quest to Find the Silver Lining in Misfortune, by Roni Robbins

The Girl Who Counted Numbers. A Novel, by Roslyn Bernstein

There was a garden in Nuremberg. A Novel, by Navina Michal Clemerson

The Butterfly and the Axe, by Omer Bartov

To Live Another Day. A Novel, by Elizabeth Rosenberg

The Right to Happiness. After all they went through. Stories, by Helen Schary Motro

To Love Another Day. A Novel, by Elizabeth Rosenberg

The series **Holocaust Heritage** consists of the following memoirs by 2G:

The Cello Still Sings. A Generational Story of the Holocaust and of the Transformative Power of Music, by Janet Horvath

The Fire and the Bonfire. A Journey into Memory, by Ardyn Halter

The Silk Factory: Finding Threads of My Family's True Holocaust Story, by Michael Hickins

Winter Light. The Memoir of a Child of Holocaust Survivors, by Grace Feuerverger

Out from the Shadows. Growing up with Holocaust Survivor Parents, by Willie Handler

Hidden in Plain Sight. A Family Memoir and the Untold Story of the Holocaust in Serbia, by Julie Brill

The Unspeakable. Breaking decades of family silence surrounding the Holocaust, by Nicola Hanefeld

Better to Light a Candle than Curse the Darkness. A Novel about Loss and Recovery, by Joanna Rosenthall

Austrian Again. Reclaiming a Lost Legacy, by Anne Hand

The series **Holocaust Books for Young Adults** consists of the following novels, based on true stories:

The Boy behind the Door. How Salomon Kool Escaped the Nazis. Inspired by a True Story, by David Tabatsky

Running for Shelter. A True Story, by Suzette Sheft

The Precious Few. An Inspirational Saga of Courage based on True Stories, by David Twain with Art Twain

Dark Shadows Hover, by Jordan Steven Sher

The Sun will Shine on You again one Day, by Cynthia Monsour

The series **WWII Historical Fiction** consists of the following novels, some of which are based on true stories:

Mendelevski's Box. A Heartwarming and Heartbreaking Jewish Survivor's Story, by Roger Swindells

A Quiet Genocide. The Untold Holocaust of Disabled Children in WWII Germany, by Glenn Bryant

The Knife-Edge Path, by Patrick T. Leahy

Brave Face. The Inspiring WWII Memoir of a Dutch/German Child, by I. Caroline Crocker and Meta A. Evenbly

When We Had Wings. The Gripping Story of an Orphan in Janusz Korczak's Orphanage. A Historical Novel, by Tami Shem-Tov

Jacob's Courage. Romance and Survival amidst the Horrors of War, by Charles S. Weinblatt

A Semblance of Justice. Based on true Holocaust experiences, by Wolf Holles

Under the Pink Triangle. Where forbidden love meets unspeakable evil, by Katie Moore

Amsterdam Publishers Newsletter

Subscribe to our Newsletter by selecting the menu at the top (right) of **amsterdampublishers.com** or scan the QR-code below.

www.ingramcontent.com/pod-product-compliance
Lightning Source LLC
LaVergne TN
LVHW020427070526
838199LV00004B/308